UNLIKELY ALLY

UNLIKELY ALLY

HOW THE MILITARY FIGHTS CLIMATE CHANGE AND PROTECTS THE ENVIRONMENT

MARILYN BERLIN SNELL

H

HEYDAY, BERKELEY, CALIFORNIA

The publisher wishes to thank the following organizations and individuals for their generous contributions to this project: The Nature Conservancy, the California Wildlife Foundation, Tim Disney, the Roy & Patricia Disney Family Foundation, and the Endangered Habitats League.

Excerpt from "Foggy Perspective" © 2018 by Robert Thielen.
Reprinted by permission of the author.

Library of Congress Cataloging-in-Publication Data
Names: Snell, Marilyn Berlin, author.
Title: Unlikely ally : how the military fights climate change and protects the environment / Marilyn Berlin Snell.
Other titles: How the military fights climate change and protects the environment
Description: Berkeley, California : Heyday, [2018] | Includes bibliographical references.
Identifiers: LCCN 2018009692 (print) | LCCN 2018013644 (ebook) | ISBN 9781597144612 (e-pub) | ISBN 9781597144063 (hardcover : alk. paper)
Subjects: LCSH: Military bases--California--Environmental aspects. | Environmental protection--California--Case studies. | Wildlife conservation--California--Case studies. | Renewable energy sources--California--Case studies. | Climate change mitigation--United States--Case studies. | Environmental responsibility--United States--Case studies. | California--Environmental conditions.
Classification: LCC TD195.A75 (ebook) | LCC TD195.A75 S67 2018 (print) | DDC 363.738/760973--dc23
LC record available at https://lccn.loc.gov/2018009692

Cover Photo: Melnotee/Istock/Thinkstock
Book Design: Ashley Ingram
Map: David Deis

Orders, inquiries, and correspondence should be addressed to:
     Heyday
     P.O. Box 9145, Berkeley, CA 94709
     (510) 549-3564
     www.heydaybooks.com

Printed in Dexter, Michigan, by Thomson-Shore

10 9 8 7 6 5 4 3 2 1

For R and Al
and for Gregory

CONTENTS

PREFACE

PLAYING POWER GAMES
WITH A THREAT MULTIPLIER

September 8, 2011, dawned warm across the American Southwest—nothing new for the region—but by 1:57 p.m. it was 115
degrees in California's Imperial Valley, much hotter than normal for that time of year. Utility companies in these parts consider September a "shoulder" season, when customer demands
for energy are lower than in peak summer months, and often
schedule transmission-maintenance outages. Several important
transmission lines were down for repair that particular September day. When a crush of air conditioners powered up across
the Imperial Valley and electricity demand spiked, the region's
chief grid and transmission operator for the territory, Arizona
Public Service, saw the danger signs in real time. At its North
Gila substation, a critical and automatic safety measure kicked
in for devices called series capacitors, which were bypassed in
order to optimize the voltage on the utility's transmission line.

An experienced substation technician was dispatched to the
North Gila site to perform what's called "switching" to isolate
the capacitors. He was to execute eleven crucial steps that had
to be done in exact order. It was high stress, and he was both
on the phone with the APS system operator (required company

protocol for switching) and distracted by a maintenance crew he was trying to give instructions to. He missed two steps.

At 3:27 p.m. the massive transmission line that runs through the North Gila substation and carries electricity from Arizona to the Imperial Valley; Northern Baja, Mexico; and San Diego went down. About ten minutes later, residents in Yuma, Arizona, began to lose power. From there the blackout cascaded south and west, affecting more than five million people, some for up to twelve hours. All of the San Diego area lost power. According to a report by the Federal Energy Regulatory Commission: "The blackout happened near rush hour, on a business day, snarling traffic for hours. Schools and businesses closed, some flights and public transportation were disrupted, water and sewage pumping stations lost power." Marine Corps Air Station Miramar went down. So did Marine Corps Base Camp Pendleton in northern San Diego County.

The day it happened, Major General Anthony (Tony) Jackson was just two months shy of retirement after serving thirty-six years in the Marine Corps. As commanding general of Marine Corps Installations West, based at Camp Pendleton, he was the man in charge when the power went out. His command center was equipped with emergency power, and when the blackout rolled over Camp Pendleton some of his diesel generators kicked on for base headquarters. That was the "one good thing" that happened that day, Jackson said.

Jackson immediately put his base on high alert. "My HQ never lost communications within my command, but power was cut to our housing and the other facilities. We had ramifications for water supply." Power was not fully restored to the base until 4:30 a.m.

When the electrical grid goes down—whether compromised

by human error, antiquated infrastructure, natural disaster, or cyberattack—the cascading negative consequences can be profound, as those who experienced the 2011 blackout discovered. To put the need for grid security starkly, as did the authors of a 2017 paper for the Truman Center, a nationwide membership organization of veterans, policy analysts, and political advisors created in the aftermath of 9/11 to reconceptualize national security in the twenty-first century, the failure of the electrical grid "can be seen as the single point of failure to the American way of life."

Jackson understood the broader implications of being dependent on a power grid he had no control over. "If you lose communication with your satellites, if you don't have the Internet, you're in trouble and it's all interrelated with energy policy," he said. "We need to be self-sufficient so we can do the business of national security."

Diesel generators kept Jackson's HQ lit and connected during the massive electricity-system failure. But he didn't want to depend on fossil fuels for backup going forward. He wanted the US military—the world's largest single petroleum buyer—to wean itself from its dependence on fossil fuels. This was by no means a radical idea: The federal law that set the Defense Department goal to "procure or produce" no less than 25 percent renewable energy for its facilities by 2025 was signed by President George W. Bush in 2007. After leading the initial campaigns in Afghanistan and Iraq in the early days of those wars, General James Mattis—now Donald Trump's secretary of defense—called on the Defense Department to "unleash us from the tether of fuel." The Marine Corps alone was consuming in excess of 200,000 gallons of fuel per day in Afghanistan during the height of that war. Mattis's comments came as the army was losing an average of two soldiers for every fifty fuel-supply convoys.

"It was during the war in Afghanistan that there was a very clear recognition that the fuel-supply lines were leading to a huge number of deaths and injuries, and that the nexus between security and energy was very real," a former Pentagon official working on energy initiatives told me.

In a speech to the Society of American Military Engineers a few months before the blackout, Jackson—a decorated two-star general and one of the highest-ranking African Americans in the Marine Corps—challenged his audience to think bigger and do better when it came to their role in supporting the military's mission. He called for a focus on renewable-energy development that would make the nation's need to do battle in oil-producing countries a thing of the past.

Jackson had been a young major in 1990, and was only two weeks into his new post at the National Military Command Center's Europe, Middle East, and Africa desk in the Pentagon when he got "the call," he said. At first he could not understand the thick accent on the other end of the line, so Jackson asked the man to slow down and repeat himself. "'The Iraqis. The Iraqis. They are here. This is the American Embassy in Kuwait City. Listen!'" Jackson said he could imagine the frightened man putting the phone to the embassy window. "And then I hear the rat a tat tat of machine gun fire."

The general did not even glance at the notes he'd carried to the podium. With his Marine Corps camouflage rolled into wide cuffs over his biceps, he was all business as he leaned closer to the microphone. "Two weeks into my Pentagon tour we were at war in the Middle East and we haven't stopped. A generation has been born since then, and graduated college, and we're still there. We didn't get the [lines at gas stations] of the 1970s. We didn't get the threat when Iraq invaded Kuwait. We seem to be continually willing to spill American blood. Our scientists, our engineers, have not devoted the same effort to conserving and producing energy as was expended on the Manhattan Project for the atom bomb."

In his way, Jackson was just trying to get help following orders: The commandant of the Marine Corps had identified energy as a top priority, setting a goal of increasing renewable-energy consumption by 2020 and echoing others in Pentagon leadership who had announced that energy independence was a priority both at home and abroad. Jackson was also in sync with the state of California. Since 2002, California has had one of the most ambitious renewable-energy policies in the nation. The Renewables Portfolio Standard, passed in Sacramento with bipartisan support, required electric utilities to increase their procurement of renewable-energy resources to 20 percent by 2017. Governor Jerry Brown upped that already impressive ante in his 2015 inaugural address when he called for California to increase its renewables portfolio to 50 percent by 2030.

Since coming to Camp Pendleton in 2009, Jackson had led the charge for all seven of the Marine Corps bases under his command in the western region to ramp up their ability to produce renewable energy. For him, on-site renewable-energy generation was a win-win and a no-brainer: In an emergency that knocked out power to the electricity grid his bases could "island" and produce their own power independently; renewable-energy generation would also reduce the need for oil from places that didn't much care for the United States.

Yet even with the winds of change at Jackson's back, and pushes of support from his military higher-ups and the

California legislature, at every critical juncture in his quest to expand on-base renewable-power generation he was met with insurmountable obstacles to success.

WHILE I WAS REPORTING FOR THIS BOOK, current commanding generals and directors of public works at Southern California installations I visited expressed a contemporaneous version of General Jackson's early frustrations: They'd get a few small renewable-energy projects green-lighted and built but then hit a wall of restrictions. Captain Rich Wiley, the commander of Naval Air Weapons Station China Lake, was among the first to voice a complaint, telling me that, "Even though we have the capacity to generate more power, we can't. [We have] limits on our ability to produce renewable energy and provide for the base." He mentioned something called Rule 21 when talking about the limit, but he could not explain what it was.

To be honest, Wiley's protestations initially struck me as a snow job: a military leader with a crisp khaki flight suit and Robert Redford looks saying that though he *wanted* to generate more renewable power on base, he couldn't? Really? Since when had the military started channeling the Sierra Club?

Yet, on a tour of a small solar array near the fence line at China Lake the next day, the base's Utilities and Energy Management branch head Robert Campos complained about the mysterious restriction as well, saying, "It's a California thing, so all the bases in the state are going to have to deal with it."

Variations on this theme were repeated at Twentynine Palms and at Fort Irwin, where the chief for Master Planning said the base could easily be "energy independent" but for "laws that keep us from generating that much power." One engineer also mentioned an obscure piece of legislation, California Senate Bill (SB) 83, as a culprit but couldn't tell me how or why.

If the military leadership and engineers at these installations had the will, the know-how, and, in some cases, the environmental permits, why in the world would they be unable to build out renewables capacity? Especially those bases in the Mojave Desert that had thousands of acres of already disturbed land (which could make environmental permitting easier, and opposition from conservation groups less intense) and almost perfectly constant supplies of daytime solar power? It didn't make sense.

I asked several California energy experts who stated confidently that there were no explicit numerical limits on renewable-energy generation. One in particular noted that in a hard-fought battle in Sacramento between California's progressive legislature and the state's investor-owned utilities, renewable-energy advocates had prevailed: Passed in 2013, California Assembly Bill (AB) 327 is landmark energy legislation that lifts the 1-megawatt cap on "customer-sited renewable generation" that had bedeviled the Marine Corps' Tony Jackson. The common term for this kind of generation is "net energy metering" or "net metering"; it allows customers with solar arrays to export excess energy during the day and get the same number of kilowatt-hours back over the course of the year. With the 2013 passage of AB 327, net metering was allowed for larger systems—with the details, including any cap on system size, to be worked out by regulators at the California Public Utilities Commission. I was told that this victory means that these systems could potentially produce up to 100 percent of their on-site power needs with renewable energy. There is no carve-out military cap in AB 327, they told me. However, the law left it to the regulators to set a cap if the PUC felt it was necessary. If one took her eyes off the ball at AB

327, she'd think the military guys didn't know what they were talking about.

The whole thing seemed like a wild-goose chase, but in a last-ditch effort before turning to other things I contacted someone who works at the nexus between utilities and solar power companies on interconnection issues (and whose proximity to these power players led him to ask, for reasons that will soon become clear, that I not use his name). He is well versed in the subject and an expert on Rule 21 and net energy metering.

ELECTRIC RULE 21, as it's formally known, has been around a long time, it turns out. First adopted by the California Public Utilities Commission in 1982—several decades before the state began incentivizing and actively promoting the wide deployment of rooftop solar and other types of renewable-energy generation—Rule 21 laid the groundwork for how non-utility-owned generating facilities interconnected their decentralized, or "distributed," generation with the electrical grid. As the distributed generation of renewables mushroomed, the complexity of technical and policy issues increased as well. Rule 21 has morphed along the way to try and keep up. In 2013, AB 327 directed the Public Utilities Commission to revise its net metering and Rule 21 rules yet again; allowed that the commission could lift the 1-megawatt cap; and directed that the cost of interconnecting larger facilities under Rule 21 be passed along to the customer.

Very few producers of renewable power—solar, wind, biomass, or fuel cell—are truly "off the grid," meaning completely disconnected and independent from their local electric-power provider. Renewable energy is intermittent, while most consumers want electricity on demand. Given that fact, how much should "self-generating" customers pay for interconnection, and for the operation and upkeep of the electrical grid upon which they continue to depend? Should there be some fixed charges they can't avoid, so as to ensure that those who can't afford to (or don't want to) put solar panels on their roofs, et cetera, don't get costs shifted onto them? How much should utilities pay for the customer-generated renewable power put onto the grid? Should it be the retail price, so that if customers use at home exactly as much power as they put on the grid, the net cost of their electricity would be $0? If they put more on than they use, how much credit should they receive? The Public Utilities Commission was given direction in AB 327 to answer such questions, then set up its rulemaking schedule and reached its final decisions on these quite complicated and fiercely contested matters in 2016.

The timing of these various rules and regulations is important, so please hang in there.

The Public Utilities Commission issued its new net energy metering rules in January 2016—the result of the process that started after the passage of AB 327. The new rules included the surprise that net metering would be capped only by the customer's load, meaning that a customer could now generate as much electricity per year as he or she was expected to consume. California produces 44 percent of all the distributed solar power generated in the United States, so the rules of engagement set in motion by 2013's AB 327 and codified in the commission's establishment of new net energy metering rules matter a great deal. As California goes, so goes the nation.

But as the Public Utilities Commission was transparently going through its rulemaking and decision-making process, a powerful shadow group was deliberating over the net metering terms as well—a group powerful enough to handicap the military's ability to fully participate in California's renewable-energy revolution.

If not for the help of the net metering and Rule 21 expert, I would never have been able to figure this out.

OVER THE PHONE with this expert, I read transcripts from conversations I'd had with base commanders and public works directors. Did these military guys have a legitimate beef? I asked. He said he'd just completed an 8-megawatt interconnection deal with no problem, then added, "The net energy metering rules allow considerably larger systems than that. I haven't looked at the military base issue, but essentially you can do a system of unlimited size," to offset on-site load. He was confident that the military men had been mistaken. The PUC's final decision was a good outcome, he said, since it streamlined the application process for distributed generation, provided a level playing field regardless of the size of the renewable power project, and made the rules uniform. Toward the end of the conversation, he apologized for not being able to help more but underscored that the new net energy metering rules were a friend and not a foe to renewable-energy producers.

Case closed, I thought. So, I was surprised when I heard from him a few days later. His curiosity piqued by the inquiry, he'd undertaken a deeper dive. His email began: "Regarding the NEM [net energy metering] rules for military facilities, there's a crazy sequence of events that I'll try to explain."

The bottom line: California military installations *do* have a 12-megawatt cap on renewable-power generation, and the source of that one-size-fits-all restriction was indeed SB 83, just as one of the military's engineers had told me. Virtually no other renewable-energy producer in the state has such a restriction, and it wasn't accidental.

Senate Bill 83 was a seventy-three-page omnibus bill signed into law by Governor Jerry Brown in 2015—after the passage of the landmark AB 327 energy legislation but before the PUC's decision-making process had been completed. There is no mention of the military or its energy-generation needs in seventy-two-plus pages, but then, plunked into exactly two paragraphs, the military's renewable-energy generation is capped; its ability to export any excess power back onto the grid is effectively denied and, just to make sure, it's stipulated that installations won't be compensated if they do export power. In a final turn of the screw, it is mandated that installations will pay for any and all upgrades to the grid deemed necessary to accommodate what little self-generated power they are allowed to produce.

In 2012, an analysis conducted for the Defense Department found that solar energy development on seven DoD installations in Southern California could generate 7,000 megawatts of "technically feasible and financially viable" solar power. For comparison, between 2007 and 2016 more than 550,000 investor-owned-utility customers in California have gone solar, mostly on residential rooftops, to produce 4,500 megawatts. The military installations in California could generate one and half times as much renewable energy for public consumption as all of the residents with solar panels put together.

Given the military's renewable-power-producing potential, had language restricting it been contained in AB 327 there would likely have been pushback. The absence of that language from the relevant legislation may explain why those energy analysts I spoke with at first felt confident insisting the cap didn't exist.

It's important to remember that AB 327 was passed in 2013, but the Public Utilities Commission didn't finalize its new net metering rules until 2016, so there was no telling when SB 83 passed in 2015 that the commission would ultimately allow net metering facilities of any size so long as the customer's generation over the year will be less than his or her load. As a matter of fact, when AB 327 passed, many of those who paid attention to such things expected that the PUC would eventually set a new system-size cap of perhaps a few megawatts. So, SB 83's net metering provision that military bases could produce as much as 12 megawatts of renewable energy seemed like a big gift to the installations at the time. There was also a surprising limitation in SB 83, though: The military would get no compensation for energy exported from the base. Unlike other net metering customers, a military base could not send out energy during the day and get an equal amount back at night.

One has to know where to look for the language and then cross-reference SB 83 with other bills and PUC code sections to fully understand how the military was culled from the rest of California's eligible customer-generators. When the PUC published its decision in 2016 it appeared as if any system of any size was uncapped as long as those systems were intended to offset on-site load. Wrong. Contained therein was a special provision for military installations, based on SB 83. The statute that directed the PUC to set up new net metering rules (let's call them NEM 2.0) said that the PUC had to use the old definition of "eligible customer-generator," except that it could allow systems larger than 1 megawatt. However, the old definition included the SB 83 restriction, meaning that systems on military bases couldn't exceed 12 megawatts.

The expert I consulted thinks it's a mistake on the PUC's part to lash the military to the 12-megawatt cap in its 2016 decision while uncapping the limit for everyone else. After all, the statute says NEM 2.0 should allow for systems over 1 megawatt, without referencing the military cap in the old rules, and the spirit of the statute is to promote renewable energy. But according to several people with knowledge of the off-the-books negotiations who spoke on background, flowing the military cap through to NEM 2.0 was intentional. Because Rule 21 was updated based on these decisions, and so included the military cap, it's understandable why the military personnel I spoke with thought Rule 21 was the culprit.

A WORD ABOUT legislative shenanigans: Representatives to the California State Senate and Assembly were elected to those deliberative bodies to deliberate. But for decades there has been a work-around in the form of "budget trailer bills." Like those cute Airstreams attached to vehicles by a trailer hitch, policy proposals can be attached to budget bills in a way that allows the party in the majority to fast-track pet agendas without the hassle of having to go through the normal vetting process. Legislators can include almost anything they want to in a trailer bill; it just has to be connected in some way to the state's budget.

SB 83 passed as a budget trailer bill. The hitchhiking paragraphs relevant to the amount of renewable energy military installations were allowed to produce did not go through the normal committee process, and I'd wager that most of the legislators who voted on that unwieldy bill did not understand its implications. The authors of those paragraphs were interest-group representatives and the legislative staff members that work closely with those groups. As most grown-ups know, legislation is often written or at least heavily influenced by inter-ested parties. But the military cap seemed to me contrary to the stated renewable-energy goals of Governor Brown and the state legislature's purported support for those goals. And it did not pass the smell test, as the language was inserted into a trailer bill so as to avoid a full airing of the policy implications, as one knowledgeable source conceded to me. This person now regrets the move, but the damage has been done. The question is: Can it be undone?

AFTER MORE THAN A YEAR struggling to understand whether and then why there is a cap on the military's ability to deploy more renewable energy on its installations, I figured that the governor—whose legacy will stand firmly upon his climate change initiatives—would have the answer. Or, if he was unaware of the cap, I thought maybe someone should clue him in.

I seized my chance one August day in 2017 in Sacramento, where I was attending the All California Defense Summit, an annual gathering of policy makers and military installation and operations commanders. The surprise speaker for the close-out ceremony was Governor Brown, who received a standing ova-tion as he made his way to the podium. He talked about global instability and the recent hurricane that had taken lives and deluged Houston. With typical Brownian flourish, he threw in some philosophizing from *The Art of War*: "You remember Sun Tzu? He said one of the things you've got to know about, besides knowing your strength and knowing your enemy: he said you've got to know about the weather."

When he finished his remarks, I maneuvered my way past military brass and his security detail and told him I was working on a book on the military in California and its leadership on environmental initiatives and energy innovation. "And I came across this problem," I said. "The installations have a cap on how much renewable energy they can produce."

"Cap? What cap?" he asked.

"They have a 12-megawatt cap, and the commanding generals I talked to..." He cut me off.

"Who put the cap on them?"

"The legislature."

"All right, then we will find out how to take that cap off. That's important," he said.

THE DEFENSE SUMMIT was sponsored by the Governor's Military Council, formed by Governor Brown to advise him and the California State Legislature on national security and defense policy. Such advice may no longer be a straightforward proposition under a Trump administration that denies the existence of climate change, alas.

The US Defense Department's most recent *Quadrennial Defense Review* (2014) refers to climate change as a "threat multiplier" and lays out the stakes: "The impacts of climate change may increase the frequency, scale, and complexity of future missions.... Our actions to increase energy and water security, including investments in energy efficiency, new technologies, and renewable energy sources, will increase the resiliency of our installations and help mitigate [negative climate change] effects."

If left unchecked, the report warned, climate change could aggravate "poverty, environmental degradation, political instability, and social tensions—conditions that can enable terrorist activity and other forms of violence."

With regard to home-turf susceptibilities, in 2017 the DoD reported findings of assessments begun in 2014 on the vulnerability of installations to coastal erosion, flooding, and drought related to extreme-weather events. The document, *Climate-Related Risk to DoD Infrastructure: Initial Vulnerability Assessment Survey*, found that of the 3,500 individual DoD sites worldwide, the highest number of reported effects resulted from drought (782), followed closely by wind (763) and non-storm-surge-related flooding (706). Extreme temperatures (351) and flooding due to storm surge (225) also posed threats. Although some installations are vulnerable to more than one climate-related effect, overall the survey found that about 50 percent of the installations are at risk.

Military personnel told me on background, however, that the "tone" and approach to climate change and renewable energy are different in the respective armed services now. It did not escape my notice that the navy's Renewable Energy Program Office is now called the Resilient Energy Program Office, a word tweak that opens the door for greenhouse-gas-emitting diesel and natural gas.

Acting Assistant Secretary of the Navy for Energy, Installations and Environment Steven Iselin, a career civil servant, said that in the Trump era the navy is "not opposed to renewables, but if a project doesn't contribute to resiliency then it's not something [we want] to do, so we'll have to think about how we adjust some of our renewable projects to make sure they also meet the resiliency litmus test." When I pushed him and asked what, exactly, constituted this new "resiliency litmus test," he could not say.

What can be said is that the 2014 *QDR* is still the main public document describing the United States' military doctrine and mission, and it puts climate change front and center. It follows then that any argument to lift the cap on renewable-energy generation on California's military installations should focus on the military mission and climate change as well.

One of the authors of the 2017 Truman Center white paper that stated the failure of the electrical grid "can be seen as the single point of failure to the American way of life," Andreas Mueller, is the executive director of the Governor's Military Council. Mueller is also chief of federal policy for the California Military Department, a role that entails overseeing national security policy in Governor Brown's Washington, D.C., office. Certainly, Mueller and his staff can make the argument that part of the military mission is combatting climate change. In Governor Brown they have an advocate for lifting the cap. I've got him on tape saying so.

SEVERAL PEOPLE WHO either participated in or have knowledge of how the military cap and the broader net energy metering changes came about acknowledge that a "fix" is needed. They have some good ideas. The Public Utilities Commission can reopen the debate regardless of whether the time allotted to contest its final decision has passed.

Renewable-energy interconnection issues are as complicated as three-dimensional chess and highly technical. But the decision to limit the role of military installations in California's renewable-energy revolution is an inelegant if not underhanded move. As to the cap itself, according to someone with knowledge of the negotiations, an impasse was broken and the number 12 was agreed upon when one party was missing an ally and everyone wanted to be done with the haggling. Partisans were told that this was the best it was going to get.

This does not seem an appropriate means by which a decision affecting all of California—hell, the entire planet—should be made. Twelve is an utterly capricious number: The Marine Corps Air Station Miramar needs about 14 megawatts to offset its on-site load, for example. Larger installations like Camp Pendleton need much more.

Forget for a moment that bad decisions were made. It's enough to know how they were made to argue that those original stakeholders should get back to the drawing board and try again, but this time more transparently and accompanied by independent energy analysts and technical experts. It's time: Regulators speculate that by the mid-2020s over 85 percent of the state's electricity load will be taken care of either by self-generation or by sources other than the large investor-owned utilities in California. At this rate, uncapped generation on military installations will be the least of the utilities' worries.

1. **ARMY NATIONAL TRAINING CENTER FORT IRWIN**

2. **NAVAL AIR WEAPONS STATION CHINA LAKE**

3. **MARINE CORPS AIR STATION MIRAMAR**

4. **SAN CLEMENTE ISLAND RANGE COMPLEX**

5. **MARINE CORPS AIR GROUND COMBAT CENTER TWENTYNINE PALMS**

6. **MARINE CORPS BASE CAMP PENDLETON**

Eureka

Redding

SIERRA

Sacramento

Lake Tahoe

San Francisco

NEVADA

Monterey

Bishop

DEATH

VALLEY

N.P.

San Luis Obispo

Ridgecrest

Other Military Installations

Urbanized Areas [Southern CA]

Santa Barbara

Barstow

Baker

MOJAVE

Needles

Los Angeles

CHANNEL

Twentynine Palms

DESERT

JOSHUA TREE N.P.

Temecula

Oceanside

ISLANDS

Salton Sea

San Diego

Temecula

Margarita River

Santa

Oceanside

Pacific Ocean

INTRODUCTION

The US military is the planet's dominant war-fighting machine. Each year, it spends more on defense and international security than China, Russia, the United Kingdom, France, Japan, India, Saudi Arabia, Germany, and Canada combined. A generous portion of that $611 billion pie goes to help make the men and women of America's armed services among the best trained in the world.

Much of the training happens in Southern California: amidst the waters, estuaries, sage scrub, and oak groves of the Pacific coast; in the inhospitable desolation of the Mojave Desert; and in San Diego, the eighth-largest city in the United States. Young recruits learn to fire M16 assault rifles and M4 carbines. They learn how to spot IEDs and murder holes. They learn how to read maps, drive tanks, take orders, and blow things up. Victory is their mission. As one former marine told me, "We don't train to lose."

An opaque, hierarchical, and testosterone-driven world, the military is not known for environmental sensitivities. So I was skeptical when, in 2006, a field organizer for the Sierra Club, where I worked as staff writer for *Sierra*, suggested I profile

Major General Michael Lehnert of the Marine Corps for the magazine. At the time, Lehnert was base commander at Camp Pendleton and regional commander of all seven Marine Corps installations west of the Mississippi. He was a two-star general in a nation at war. He was also an advocate for robust environmental stewardship on Department of Defense lands.

California and the DoD make for interesting bedfellows: The military presence in the state contributed nearly $50 billion to the economy in 2015—more than the computer and electronics industry or the motion pictures and music juggernaut. The state's unique and vast natural environments help sustain military readiness by providing realistic settings to hone fighting skills in advance of real combat. Those environments also sustain rich natural resources: Southern California contributes heavily to the larger California Floristic Province, one of the twenty-five most biologically diverse regions in the world, and it contains significant numbers of threatened and endangered species protected by federal and state law.

Lehnert presided over an installation with eighteen threatened and endangered species. When I visited, he and I toured the Crucible. A kind of *Survivor* experience for marines, the Crucible is a last-stop, sixty-hour outdoor endurance test before deployment. Among the most impressive survivors at the Crucible, however, are little mammals no longer than your thumb. The Pacific pocket mouse has been pummeled nearly to extinction by its affection for habitat along Southern California's coastline, most of which has been bulldozed for housing development. Reduced to three colonies on all of planet Earth, two of those colonies were located on Camp Pendleton's relatively undeveloped expanse. Standing at the Crucible, we were at ground zero for one of them. Military exercises had been designed to ensure that training at the Crucible did not push the species closer to the brink. "It's possible," Lehnert told me that day, "to find ways to get marines ready for combat and at the same time be good stewards. It's not a zero-sum game to me." Since the Lehnert profile more than ten years ago, climate change has been officially acknowledged—first by Governor Arnold Schwarzenegger and then by Governor Jerry Brown—as having a significant and measurable impact on California's environment and therefore DoD installations in the state.

That mission readiness and environmental stewardship can coexist is counterintuitive, like hearing death metal blare from a minivan. But coexistence is not merely aspirational. It's the law, and it applies to all military installations on US territory. *How* those laws are applied—perfunctorily or full throttle—varies from base to base. A few in Southern California have seized the challenge and taken a more comprehensive approach, one in which energy security and natural and cultural resource protection are embedded in the concept of national defense. Those are the bases I chose to focus on for this book.

THE STUDY OF NATURE has been a survival strategy since the Neanderthals 250,000 years ago. It's also a defensive art. During World War I, French Impressionist painters traveled to the front as "camouflage inspectors" to study color, taking note of dominant and recessive tones in nature and then translating their sketches onto the fabric of troop uniforms so that those wearing them could blend in to the countryside. The first "frog-skin" camouflage, designed during World War II for the US Marine Corps, was created by a horticulturist and gardening editor for *Better Homes and Gardens.* Camouflage works because it breaks patterns and blurs borders in a manner that allows its wearer to become part of nature's matrix. What's more, it reveals through visual trickery a fundamental truth about interdependence.

Wildlife and habitat protection was not on the minds of those who drove California's great military land grab. If the gold rush ignited the boom that would forever transform the northern part of the state, the bombing of Pearl Harbor and US entry into World War II forever changed its southern half. Fueled by threats real and imagined, vast ranchos, little-used airstrips, and sparsely populated desert landscapes were all converted by decree into Department of Defense properties. Even with the base realignment and closures that have decommissioned upward of 350 installations nationwide, more than two-thirds of all Marine Corps training continues to take place in Southern California's Mojave Desert, for instance.

With the population of this region continuing its robust growth, military installations have become de facto refuges for threatened and endangered species—in the Mojave, at Camp Pendleton, and elsewhere. These installations have been successful in preserving threatened and endangered species, but the tactics used have not been without controversy. When a species is listed, land essential to that species' conservation is often put out of bounds to anything that adversely modifies it. For the military, that meant huge swaths of "critical habitat" could be placed off-limits to training units.

The 2004 National Defense Authorization Act granted certain critical habitat exemptions from the Endangered Species Act for military installations. Bases can now implement plans that address entire ecosystems rather than having to focus on carved-out bits of habitat. Ecosystem management is far more complex than managing a plot of land for one species, but those charged with environmental security on the bases I visited insist it's a better means to a positive end. If I can analogize to lessons learned in Iraq and Afghanistan, the military's reasoning would go something like this: Don't throw all your weight and resources at one village while ignoring the wider context and complex interrelationships.

Twenty years of solid data support the military's contention that it is possible to take an integrated rather than a targeted approach. At Pendleton, one of the world's largest colonies of endangered California least terns has grown from several hundred pairs to more than a thousand pairs under ecosystem management, for instance.

The military has also shown success teaming up with environmental groups, mostly to fight urban encroachment. Utilizing funds made available by Congress, the Mojave Desert Land Trust and other conservation groups joined forces with the Marine Corps Air Ground Combat Center in Twentynine Palms to buy up and preserve land in perpetuity. The Gateway Parcel is now open to the public and affords unfettered views of the adjacent Joshua Tree National Park. The purchase helps the Marines create an additional buffer near the base and also creates a corridor that erases boundaries and allows wildlife, including the endangered desert tortoise, to travel less perturbed on its desired path.

Researchers at Department of Defense installations have been studying the desert tortoise on DoD lands in the Mojave for decades in an effort to bolster the population. Beyond helping with the design of wildlife corridors, research inquiries into how the animal flushes toxins and retains water during a drought could improve our understanding of how to survive a trip to Mars. In myth the world is carried through the universe on a turtle's back. In the Mojave Desert tortoise, we glimpse how this ancient animal actually could help us travel through space.

Water is the holy grail of the desert and, increasingly, for all of California, whose years of drought may be the new normal in a world transformed by climate change. Accommodating to this altered state of nature is also a survival strategy. At the army's National Training Center at Fort Irwin, north of Barstow, engineers have just brought on line a facility that will double the life of its aquifer and therefore the base. Fort Irwin is essentially carrying us all through what investors call the "Valley of Death," showing proof of concept and viability and therefore making it more likely that technologies such as those at the Irwin Water Works will be utilized in thirsty cities across the American West. Similar to the Defense Department's research and development investment in the early Internet and the technology that led to GPS, the army's considerable expenditure on this project could pay incalculable peace dividends.

Fort Irwin's neighbor just to the west is Naval Air Weapons Station China Lake, where scientists are developing clean-burning and renewable rocket fuels made from cedar extracts. Developing fuels that create fewer of the greenhouse gases that contribute to climate change is not a side benefit of defense work; it's a strategic imperative given a geopolitical landscape easily destabilized by the effects of climate change. When it comes to extreme weather and its cataclysmic outcomes, there are no borders. There is no us and them. Both bases could do much more on the climate action front by increasing their renewable-energy generation, with commanders and public works directors there telling me that energy security is a priority for them. First, though, constraints on how many megawatts military installations can produce must be lifted.

A potentially disruptive technology is also taking shape at Marine Corps Air Station Miramar, which has turned its cramped quarters within the urban sprawl of greater San Diego into an asset—teaming up with the city on forward-leaning energy and water infrastructure. Air station property leased to the City of San Diego for a landfill is now producing large quantities of renewable energy, some of it going to the base and some of it going to power a new and advanced water treatment facility that will in a few years satisfy one-third of the area's drinking water needs. The partnership is showing us what sustainable twenty-first-century public works projects can look like.

In *The Art of War*, Sun Tzu counseled his adherents to "plan for what is difficult while it is easy, do what is great while it is small." The sage of sixth-century-BC China described how conflict could be mitigated or even avoided altogether by understanding its inflection points and accelerants. The modern American military's drive to bolster resiliency among vulnerable populations of flora and fauna, so as to avoid mandated regulatory interventions down the line, points toward a new concept of defense that resonates beyond environmental protection. What does "national security" mean in the twenty-first century? Increasingly, it means building resiliency in vulnerable human populations and mitigating climatic disruptions that drive mass displacement through droughts, floods, resource scarcity, and, eventually, failed states.

This is a book about leadership. The military takes pride in being the tip of the spear when it comes to war-fighting. Across the Southern California landscape, it's also a trailblazer in the environmental research and practice of building resiliency and nurturing life.

CHAPTER 1

THE BATTLE FOR NET ZERO

ARMY NATIONAL TRAINING CENTER FORT IRWIN

Take a guess at which Southern California municipalities struggle with water scarcity, power outages, maxed-out landfills, and interests that hinder creative problem solving and sustainable innovation, and odds are you're right: Most towns in the region suffer one or all of these plagues. Now, imagine a center for innovation that is attempting to fight through the encumbrances of short-term thinking and perceived limits of technology to create a sustainable model for resource-constrained urban life. Imagine a place that strives to set the standard—to embody "proof of concept"—and has been engaged in Herculean efforts to bring on line some of the most promising green technology around.

If you're stumped, Google "middle of nowhere California." The first series of hits are spot on: One advertises a sky-blue T-shirt emblazoned with "Middle of Nowhere Fort Irwin" (it's going for $19.99). Another is a YouTube post by an army spouse documenting her and her husband's cross-country road trip to the base. After passing from Texas through New Mexico and Arizona, the video shows a vast, empty expanse with a few creosote bushes and a whole lot of sun-bleached dirt. A caption reads

"Middle of Nowhere," and a voice that sounds slightly freaked out intones, "Fort Irwin. Ugh. Look at this!"

The base's total population of around twenty-four thousand consists of four to five thousand rotational soldiers and approximately seven thousand family members; military personnel assigned to the base plus a civilian workforce make up the rest. The army's National Training Center at Fort Irwin is tethered to California's already shaky power grid by what the base's public works director, Muhammad Bari, has not-altogether-hyperbolically called "one 30-mile-long extension cord." All it takes is a tree striking the power line to knock out electricity to the entire base, something that's happened before. During a national crisis such as a natural disaster or terrorist attack, a prolonged power outage at the energy-insecure base could be catastrophic.

Fort Irwin is also water constrained; it's in a part of the Mojave Desert that sees fewer than 5 inches of measurable rain per year on average. Generally, a desert is defined as an area that gets fewer than 10 inches per year, so Fort Irwin can rightly be considered serious desert. Its northern boundary almost touches Death Valley, the country's hottest, driest, and lowest national park.

Upon arrival at the 1,000-square-mile base, I receive a fluorescent-orange card—bright enough to find on my person when preoccupied with being lost but small enough to fit in a wallet. The card contains the "ten commandments" of desert survival, from #1: "Hold on to a survival attitude"; to #3: "Move only when absolutely necessary and only at night"; to #8: "Keep your mouth closed (Breathe through your nose to minimize evaporative water loss)"; to #10: "Use your head, not your sweat—drink the water you have." That is, if you have any water left.

As much grief as Fort Irwin receives for being a remote and

treacherous outpost of human civilization, its harsh surroundings provide a realistic environment for soldiers to train in. Each month for ten months of the year, often in sweltering temperatures above 100 degrees, the base conducts live-fire as well as force-on-force, brigade-size training on its various ranges (a brigade is between three thousand and five thousand soldiers). In these exercises, rotational troops from other army installations often go up against Fort Irwin's active-duty personnel. As much as possible, the training simulates the tempo, breadth, and intensity of current conflicts. Units trained at Fort Irwin are sent to Afghanistan, Iraq, and Kuwait but also to Europe and South Korea, and on domestic missions. In 2012 active-duty soldiers trained at Fort Irwin deployed for rescue and recovery operations after Hurricane Sandy's devastation along the eastern seaboard. In 2017 they were sent to Houston for Hurricane Harvey relief.

To help train realistically, Fort Irwin has constructed 15 mini cities with as many as 585 buildings at one site. In army speak they're referred to as MOUTs, Military Operations on Urbanized Terrain sites. Some have working, man-size tunnels; some have buildings five stories tall; and some have facsimile open sewers that emit the malodorous affronts experienced by many soldiers sent abroad. The combat towns, currently with names like Ujen and Tiefort City, feature mosques and public address systems amplifying music and Arabic calls to prayer. In the parlor of a mock hotel in Ujen, a hookah and tea set greet the visitor. The towns can morph almost overnight to look, feel, and smell like the next geopolitical hot spot.

During my visit to Ujen one April morning, army tacticians make final adjustments before the day's urban-combat exercise begins. Arabic-speaking actors hired by the base are stationed at roadside stands and prepare to hawk fruits, vegetables, and other goods. My army handler, Ken Drylie, informs me that military spouses will also be observing the exercise, so it will be "much tamer than usual, not the realistic training soldiers usually get." There will not, for example, be amputee actors fitted with prosthetics—their fake limbs getting realistically blown off by a facsimile improvised explosive device. "There's usually a lot of fake blood and screaming," Drylie says over the din of scratchy music and truck engines as a convoy of soldiers lumbers into Ujen. He adds that "the longer it takes to secure the wounded and get out, the worse the soldiers' lives become. More crap starts happening if they don't move fast enough."

The actors have a loose script and play a variety of good guys, mayors, insurgents, people who just don't like American military personnel—every kind of character, Drylie explains. "The script tells you who you are, who your relatives are and where they live, what their attitudes are, what your attitudes are. Your attitude changes based on interactions with the training unit. Say you're my cousin and you live in one village and I live in another. Everything's going great with me and the training unit in my village, but you're getting roughed up by the training unit in your village. I find out about it and now I'm mad. The soldiers need to figure out why." Not all the conversations are in English, so interpreters are also thrown into the mix. "The important thing is you've got to learn not to piss everybody off. There's a balancing act. You've got to take out the bad guys but make sure you take care of the good guys."

The violence that ensues in the demonstration is G-rated but still unnerving: As the army convoy passes beneath the bridge where we stand, an IED hidden in a rusted-out car nearby explodes and immediately the rapid cracks of sniper fire break out. The soldier manning one of the convoy's Jeep-mounted assault rifles "fires" in the direction of the sniper attack, but his target remains hidden in a building—the hotel? the residence next to it?—and keeps on firing. Villagers scream and a soldier is "hit." Anyone who tries to reach the injured man comes under heavy sniper fire. The medic unit cannot reach the area quickly, so the screaming and gunfire intensify.

"Our MOUTs provide a form of training for the army that we take very seriously, more so in recent decades in light of Afghanistan and Iraq," says Colonel G. Scott Taylor, Fort Irwin's garrison commander, when I meet him. "Our whole purpose being here is to provide a world-class training environment to our nation's army so it's prepared to deploy in harm's way." In lieu of training environments like this, soldiers would be forced to learn survival skills on the job—when the IEDs, sniper fire, and insurgents are real, he says.

This kind of training does more than save lives, according to my eighty-seven-year-old father, who's army all the way. His was a short stint in postwar Germany, 1954 to 1956, and he saw no action. Commissioned as a second lieutenant in the infantry, he left the service as a first lieutenant and often talks about how the army shaped him. "It was probably the most important and thorough learning experience of my life. I learned how to follow first and then how to lead," the retired CEO said.

Just as Fort Irwin's realistic training and harsh environment provide a chance to test one's mettle and to engage in real-world combat scenarios, it also creates the opportunity to grapple with other real-world threats, including water scarcity, energy insecurity, and climate change. In 2010 Assistant Secretary of the Army for Installations, Energy and Environment Katherine Hammack announced the creation of the Army Net Zero

Initiative, with an aim to have installations conserve water and energy, consume only as much power as renewably produced on base, and reduce to as close to zero as possible all waste, hazardous and otherwise. Faced with extreme water and energy challenges, this middle-of-nowhere military base is fighting hard to get to net zero—winning some battles and retrenching after others to prepare to fight another day.

FORT IRWIN'S—AND, BY EXTENSION, THE US MILITARY'S—forward thinking was not always thus. Legislation passed in 1976 to create a legal framework for properly managing hazardous waste, for example, didn't put much of a dent in the Defense Department's behavior or its practice of ignoring properties it had despoiled in the past—a fact that became clear through the work of the 1988 Base Realignment and Closure Commission. The goal of the commission was to save the Pentagon millions of dollars by consolidating or closing underutilized installations and then selling off the real estate. The problem was that the installations had been so contaminated by the hazardous by-products of nearly four decades of environmental neglect that the property couldn't even be given away.

"The military industry has produced the most toxic pollution in the country and virtually every military installation has been extensively contaminated," the *New York Times* reported in 1991. The front-page article, by Keith Schneider, noted that hazardous chemicals had been tossed into lagoons or merely dumped on the ground, only to seep into water supplies that spread the poisons more widely. Since federal law prohibited the Pentagon from selling any property on bases until contamination on the entire site was cleaned up, Schneider reported, the government's moneymaking plan suddenly became a $30 billion bill to taxpayers for cleanup.

More recent investigative reporting by the independent news organization ProPublica found that this toxic legacy persists across much of the DoD-controlled landscape. In the series Bombs in Our Backyard, which began in July 2017, ProPublica's Abrahm Lustgarten reported that there are tens of thousands of "known or suspected toxic sites on 5,500 current or former Pentagon properties." He cited an Environmental Protection Agency staff estimate that the contamination covered "40 million acres—an area larger than the state of Florida—and the costs for cleaning them up will run to hundreds of billions of dollars."

The military has been able to continue the toxic practice of open burning and disposal of hazardous materials via an obscure addendum to 1976's Resource Conservation and Recovery Act, Subpart X, according to Lustgarten. What was to be an interim accommodation for the problematic treatment and disposal of explosives continues to this day. Lustgarten refers to Subpart X as a "virtual escape hatch from the rest of the law, creating the nation's open burn allowances and allowing the Department of Defense and its contractors to revert to their 1970s-era practices."

ProPublica's critique of the military holds true across most installations. Fort Irwin, too, has a legacy of profligate burning and disposal of hazardous material on the base, but that old-school behavior is no longer tolerated—a fact attributable to current leadership and some of the most stringent state environmental laws in the nation.

Colonel Taylor, forty-eight, witnessed the slow-motion train wreck of poor stewardship and bad publicity regarding the military. An army brat, Taylor spent time at Fort Irwin as a kid when his father was its commanding general and then again as a cadet. He's also witnessed the slow-motion awakening in some quarters that the military's business-as-usual strategy is a losing one: "Between the time I returned [to Fort Irwin] as a cadet in 1991 to my first rotation as a second lieutenant in 1993, the mindset changed to 'the environment matters; it's important.'"

The message that penetrated some installations came in 1991, when, for the first time, the environment was spotlighted in the *National Security Strategy of the United States*. Prepared for Congress that year by the George H. W. Bush administration, the document introduced the idea that environmental or "natural" security is integral to national security: "Global environmental concerns include such diverse but interrelated issues as stratospheric ozone depletion, climate change, food security, water supply, deforestation, biodiversity and treatment of wastes. A common ingredient in each is that they respect no international boundaries. The stress from these environmental challenges is already contributing to political conflict. Recognizing a shared responsibility for global stewardship is a necessary step for global progress. Our partners will find the United States a ready and active participant in this effort." (In 2017, climate change was dropped from the *National Security Strategy* document.)

In California, one of the most effective change agents with regard to the military's habit of carte-blanche contamination came in 1992, when the Department of Defense lost sovereign immunity. In signing the Federal Facility Compliance Act, President George H. W. Bush gave state regulators the right to access and inspect how military bases were treating, storing, and disposing of hazardous waste. The state could then impose fines and penalties for violations. California has always led the nation in formulating and enforcing muscular state environmental laws and regulations, and this federal law was a game changer for California bases like Fort Irwin. Today, the base must seek and adhere to more than a hundred state permits targeted at different locations. When state inspectors come knocking, now they always get in.

"People are surprised the army cares about the environment. They say, 'We thought you just rolled in with your multi-billion-dollar budgets and did whatever you wanted.' Growing up, I absolutely saw that. Even in my first years in the army, there was still this attitude of, 'Oh, we just spilled 150 gallons of fuel on the ground; let's kick some dirt over it.' But that's the old army. That's not our way now. We train every soldier that comes in: 'If there's a spill, you will report it. If you're caught not reporting it, there will be fines against your unit and we will go after disciplinary action against you.' We take it very seriously because it turns into poisoning our own training area and potentially our water sources and our community," Taylor says.

Justine Dishart, fifty-four, is chief of the Environmental Division of public works at Fort Irwin. A civilian now, her uniform is usually relaxed-fit jeans and, in cooler months, a fleece vest. She has a low, no-nonsense voice with a slight twang that originates perhaps in Pennsylvania, where she was born and her grandfather was a coal miner, or in Kentucky, where she spent her high school years. She's not sure: "I was raised as an army brat, all over the country."

In 1989, Dishart was already an air force veteran and recent graduate of Eastern Kentucky University when her parents called from Fort Irwin, where they worked, and told her there were jobs. "They didn't tell me it was in the middle of flippin' nowhere! I was like, 'okay.' Threw my stuff in the truck, threw the cat in the back, drove all the way out here."

She left Fort Irwin to work with the US Geological Survey in

Utah for a while but returned in 1991. "The army was standing up their environmental program and they were looking for people with geologic and hydrogeologic backgrounds," she says. She signed on as an intern then, but today she runs the division and leads a staff of ten.

Like Taylor, Dishart has watched the army change. When she returned in 1991, the base had forty-four toxic sites that required cleanup—a long and expensive process. "Sins of the past," Dishart says. Today, things are different. "We've put a lot of effort in over the years to eliminate toxics that we could eliminate and to better manage things that we could not eliminate because they were specific to a certain type of mission."

ProPublica's exposé of toxic Defense Department lands was published after I visited Fort Irwin, so I emailed Dishart and asked how the base avoided making the list of bad actors. She wrote back and said that, in general, the base has "always resisted" seeking the types of Subpart X permits that allow installations to "legally and routinely open burn/open detonate waste munitions as 'treatment.'" (Ironic single quotes hers.)

Dishart is an enforcer and has thrived in the command-and-control decision-making atmosphere of Fort Irwin. "That's one of the good things: If the commander says 'do it,' it doesn't matter if you like it or not. You've got to do it." The federal Budget Control Act of 2011 imposed across-the-board budget cuts that did not spare the Defense Department, which is why the Environmental Division's FY 2016 budget was only $10 million, Dishart says, adding that it had gone as high as $21 million in years past. (Her department is allotted seventeen staff members, a number she's not been able to reach under DoD's budgeting constraints.)

THE BASE'S HAZARDOUS MATERIAL CONTROL CENTER is not a stop on my tour I look forward to, so I'm pleasantly surprised when I am not met with throat-choking chemical smells upon arrival. The facility has a separate walk-in locker for each type of hazardous product, and everything is neatly stacked and bar-coded. When a soldier comes in to get paint, floor strippers, solvents, engine fluids—whatever is needed—his or her name and unit are entered into a database and the bar code is scanned. "This hazmat program is where Environmental started," explains Dishart, adding, "In the old days, toxic chemicals just got burned or dumped."

Dishart's team is always "OCS—out checkin' shit," she says with a laugh. For the most part, hazardous materials used on base are purchased in the facility. Rotations that bring their own hazmat must get it bar-coded so it can be tracked in the system. Unused portions aren't to be thrown away but returned—to be reissued at no cost since the material has already been paid for by another unit. If somebody engages in improper disposal and the "OCS" team finds the material, a bar-code scan can get at the source. "Most units are pretty good about handling materials. If not, my guys will find them." Hazardous waste, including used electronics, fluorescent tubing, vehicle batteries, antifreeze, and oil, is turned in at another depot, called the Pollution Prevention Yard, where it is then consolidated and shipped off base every ninety days by Chenega, a licensed contractor.

Soil contaminated by an accidental spill is trucked to the Centralized Waste Handling Facility on base, treated in a bioremediation process similar to that used after the Deepwater Horizon oil spill in the Gulf of Mexico, then used to cover the base's landfill trash.

TRASH IS A SORE SUBJECT at Fort Irwin these days. When I first visited the base in April 2016, the public works staff was excited about a $32 million waste-to-energy garbage monster that was, at the time, 90 percent completed and scheduled to fire up that June. The shiny new plant wasn't going to burn trash. It wasn't going to incinerate trash. In simple terms, the facility's core thermal-converter technology—the Pyrolytic Conversion System—was going to indirectly heat the trash, as in an Easy-Bake Oven, to between 1,600 and 1,800 degrees in the absence of oxygen to generate green electricity. The rest of the equipment was either for pollution control or part of the mechanism that would make the steam to turn the turbine to make green power.

The 5.5-acre facility was green-lighted in 2013 as part of an Energy Savings Performance Contract, a Reagan-era program tweaked during the Clinton years in which private contractors finance the up-front costs of energy-efficiency or power-generation projects at federal facilities and are repaid from estimated utility bill savings. If, for example, a federal agency was going to save $500,000 per year on its utility bill, that's how much the contractor would be paid annually to recoup its investment. Energy performance contracts like these have saved taxpayers a good deal of money. According to the Federal Energy Management Program, over the past 20 years, approximately 650 energy performance contracts worth $8 billion have been awarded to federal agencies. They have resulted in energy savings valued at almost $15 billion, of which about $11 billion went to repay project investments. That means the federal government saved nearly $4 billion on its utility bill—not to mention the savings to the planet in avoided greenhouse gas emissions.

The apparent win-win arrangement was born of the need to find innovative ways to fund energy projects and efficiency improvements in a world of both constrained budgets and increasingly ambitious government sustainability goals. As part of the DoD—the biggest energy user of any federal agency—the army is anxious to bring down costs and jumped at the chance to score an energy win at Fort Irwin with a state-of-the-art waste-to-energy plant that ate trash, generated green power, and let very few polluting emissions escape. Needless to say, the promise of a green fix for severe environmental problems is both heady and seductive, while the prospect of a massive contract underwritten by Uncle Sam has an equally powerful attraction for large corporations.

Sometimes that means government agencies take a risk and kiss a frog that transforms into something amazing. For example, an Energy Savings Performance Contract with Honeywell in 2010 resulted in a 3.9-million-square-foot campus remodel for the Food and Drug Administration that has saved millions of dollars in avoided utility, operational, and maintenance costs since it was completed in 2014. The installation of solar photovoltaic cells, improved lighting, and building envelope modifications has so far also helped the campus avoid spewing annually the equivalent of 98,000 tons of carbon dioxide into the air.

Other times, federal agencies don't see rewards—either because the project is scrapped altogether or because the promised benefits don't accrue. Trying to make the right choice on projects is highly technical and tremendously challenging. "This green space...is fraught with every kind of sales person imaginable," says Bill Walden, president and CEO of Technikon. Beginning in 2008, his company ran a Sacramento testing lab for high-temperature renewable-energy-conversion-technology validation. The lab focused on waste-to-energy and was funded by the US government and private investment. "We've run tests on systems from one end of the world to the other and rarely does the performance match the sales brochures," he says. It's an emerging technology, he adds, with prospectors racing to be the first to prove that their technology holds the (proprietary) key to net-zero waste and plentiful, cheap, and clean energy.

Fort Irwin's romance with its dreamy net-zero-waste suitors did not go well.

Testing like the kind done by Technikon and others has shown that emissions from pyrolytic conversion technologies are very low—so low that Fort Irwin did not need to obtain the requisite federal Clean Air Act permits. Before the equipment was installed, however, the technology did have to meet strict California air quality requirements and acquire a permit to construct the facility. (A permit to operate would not be granted until the facility fired up and pollution-control analyses were completed successfully.) The patent holder for the thermal converter—the place where the magic happens—was able to secure the permit to construct because she could show real data from similar technology she had been associated with.

In addition to being the founder of Integrated Energy LLC and patent holder for the Pyrolytic Conversion System, Karen Bertram is a feisty sixty-four-year-old air force veteran and entrepreneur. In a way, she has sexism to thank for her career trajectory: Toward the end of her enlistment, she attended an all-service school with members of the air force, navy, marines, and army to learn the dangerous trade of explosive ordnance disposal. Upon graduation, as she readied for EOD duty, she was told to pick another line of military work. Someone apparently decided EOD was too dangerous for a woman. (She'd been the first female to seek employment in the field.) Instead, she packed her bags and used the GI Bill to finish her education, which included studies in chemistry, physics, and linguistics as well as a JD in law from Texas Tech. While working as an investment banker in the tech sector in California, she had the insight that waste treatment was going to be a growth industry and began to explore how she could gain an edge.

In 2010, Bertram invited Fort Irwin's Muhammad Bari to a site visit at the Cabazon Band of Mission Indians lands in Riverside County, where a waste-to-energy facility using technology similar to her Pyrolytic Conversion System had been constructed. Bari was impressed by the pitch, and Bertram was invited to the base to be grilled about her system by Justine Dishart. The two women hit it off.

"Karen is a highly intelligent lady," said Dishart. "We get a lot of vendors that come through Fort Irwin trying to sell us some new technology. I've got my list of questions and they are hard. Karen was the only person who had an answer for every question I threw at her." Dishart and Bari decided they wanted Bertram's technology, but her business was far too small to handle the contract. They bid out the waste-to-energy project and Siemens Government Technologies Inc. eventually became the lead contractor—with Bertram as a subcontractor, at Fort Irwin's suggestion, supplying the essential technology.

Bertram secured the permit to construct in 2016 from the Mojave Desert Air Quality Management District, meeting the agency's "best available control technology" standard. Bertram recalls that when she got the permit from the air district "the guy said, 'People are going to hate you! Now, everybody else will need to step up because we're doing it.' We made it harder for everybody else." The air quality district's deputy director, Alan De Salvio, is not quite so effusive when describing the permit, but he does say that "anything that allows the state of California to meet its [air pollution] diversion goals is a good thing, and anything that helps diminish the waste stream is also a good thing, and this technology does both."

If Fort Irwin's waste-to-energy facility had been able to run as advertised, at full bore it would have consumed up to thirty-four tons of garbage per twenty-four-hour cycle (the base generates far less than that per day) to produce around one megawatt of electricity. Bertram's garbage monster does not consume metal or glass, but it is designed to indirectly heat everything else— even plastics, which in traditional forms of incineration produce unacceptable amounts of dioxins and furans, both known to be endocrine-disrupting and carcinogenic. "We have MREs"— meals ready to eat—"that have a lot of plastics in them. We've got targets with a high plastic component," Dishart says. All contents would have been heated in the absence of oxygen to safely decompose the materials.

What remains at the end of the pyrolytic conversion process, says Bertram, is nonhazardous char—just like the stuff in your barbecue after the coals burn down—that can be sold and recycled for use in cement, as a road base, et cetera. The facility did not require an expensive dryer at the front end of the process— needed by most waste-to-energy plants to dry the garbage before it's incinerated—because the Mojave Desert would do the work for free. Even the waste in Fort Irwin's landfill is bone dry. Dishart says they've excavated landfill trash from the 1940s and could still read the newspapers found there.

In the initial master plan for Fort Irwin, 460 acres were allotted to landfill. So far, 100 of those acres have been used. Since the waste-to-energy plant was projected to be able to handle far more trash in a day than the base produces, it would have mined waste out of the landfill—recovering acreage that could then be repurposed for training. When it ate through its own trash, Fort Irwin could then import garbage from other military installations.

"It could completely change the solid-waste paradigm. There's a lot at stake with this system," Dishart said during our first meeting. Then, the anticipation was palpable. Now, the project is kaput.

Under the terms of the agreement with the army and signed by Siemens Government Technologies, the waste-to-energy facility was to be operational by June 2015. That didn't happen, not least because the relationship between Siemens and Bertram went seriously sour and work had pretty much stopped. After failing to collect on invoices amounting to approximately $1.5 million, Bertram filed a lawsuit in September 2015 to compel the company to pay its bills. Rather than settling accounts, Siemens Government Technologies countersued, claiming that Bertram's technology was inherently flawed and so dangerous that the plant could not be operated safely, ever.

Fort Irwin was confident the spat could be reconciled and so a new date, June 2016, was set for the startup—a deadline that could have easily been met, according to Dishart. "What was left to do was [add] some switch gears, electronics—essentially control elements." But the finishing touches were never added. Instead, Siemens Government Technologies pulled the plug. Engineers hired by the respective parties disagree on the essential question of whether Bertram's core pyrolytic technology is safe, and the parties are still duking it out in court. Bertram's lawyer demanded that her technology be tested so it can be proven safe, and, as of this writing, a judge has agreed to let testing proceed. In any event, Fort Irwin and the Army Corps of Engineers, which was managing the project, grew tired of the whole business. The waste-to-energy portion of Siemens' contract with Fort Irwin has been terminated, but because it's an Energy Savings Performance Contract the army will not eat the costs. Even so, given the dashed expectations and the black mark now affixed to a promising green technology, I can't help but call it a Pyrrhic victory.

"It's certainly not the first time the government has dealt with a contract going down the toilet," responds Dishart when I say as much to her. Bari is not cowed. He's confident that the ill-fated effort is merely a road bump in his dogged pursuit of net zero. "This project failed due to unforeseen reasons that were beyond the army's control, but we are going to keep working on introducing new and emerging technology. Fort Irwin is trying to become one of the first net-zero waste installations, and utilizing this [pyrolytic conversion] technology is the key to achieve that goal." Bari's department has already initiated a process through the Defense Logistics Agency to get a new waste-to-energy project on base.

Beyond Bari's preoccupation with net-zero waste, he is even more fixated on getting as close to net-zero energy as possible. Fort Irwin requires 28 megawatts of electricity during peak summer demand. Right now, the vast majority of that electricity is provided by Southern California Edison. The base receives one monthly SCE bill, which ranges from $1.7 million a month during the summer to a low of about $631,000 during spring and fall. The electrical lifeline that connects Fort Irwin to SCE's power grid is shaky, but not that much more so than the grid itself. "[When] we are in the dark, that's a mission impact," says Bari, who takes quite seriously his responsibility for keeping the lights on.

MUHAMMAD BARI WAS BORN IN PAKISTAN, received degrees from the University of Engineering and Technology in Lahore, speaks five languages, and once volunteered to play a combat-village mayor when Fort Irwin trainers were short of brown-skinned stand-ins. He's worked on the base for more than twenty years. Colonel Taylor refers to him as an "unsung hero," while Dishart volunteers that Bari is "passionate about energy stuff." He believes in the base's training mission and is driven to find cost-effective strategies that can move it toward energy security as a means to keep training from disruption.

Bari's concerns are not theoretical: One August afternoon in 2013 a brief but ferocious thunderstorm dumped 1.8 inches of rain and knocked out Fort Irwin's power. As a rule, rainwater does not sink into the hard-packed desert soil; it flows, especially when it's coming down fast. Only ten minutes after the storm began, a flash flood was rushing down one of the base's residential streets and filling the wheel wells of parked SUVs. At base headquarters a short distance away, a half-foot wall of mud crashed into the building, and in Tiefort City, one of the large mock-combat towns, structures and monitoring equipment were impacted, rendering the town unsafe for training.

Storm repairs and future-mitigation measures cost the army $110 million. Then, a little more than two years later, another massive rainstorm hit. The offices for Marine Corps Logistics Command were badly damaged, and power to some other base facilities was knocked out for nearly two days. Since 2012, the base has experienced three major outages exceeding twenty-four hours, all of which threatened mission-critical functions.

One can be a climate-change agnostic and still acknowledge the threat that extreme weather poses to military readiness. In response to a senator's question during his 2017 confirmation hearings for secretary of defense, General James Mattis noted that the Defense Department "should be prepared to mitigate any consequences of a changing climate, including ensuring that our shipyards and installations will continue to function as required."

Bari has been trying mightily to ensure that the base has sufficient power at all times. Even before the waste-to-energy debacle, in 2009 Fort Irwin signed a deal with a multinational solar power company for a 500-megawatt project. The base would need only a fraction of the power it generated and the rest would be sold back to the grid. Clark Energy Group and Acciona Solar Power were going to build the project under an Enhanced Use Lease, which would allow the DoD to retain control over the property. "Great news for all of us and congrats to Fort Irwin for inking this great deal for the US Army and the USA," gushed a writer in the online magazine *CleanTechnica* after the deal was announced.

The 500-megawatt facility was not planned well, Bari acknowledges. "The idea started at the [army] headquarters for a 200-megawatt system and it was so promising that HQ did a small feasibility study and said we can produce 500 megawatts. They put together the initiative. But there were issues that we did not see in our crystal ball"—namely, the fact that at that time no one at Fort Irwin, or in the rest of the army, for that matter, was aware that net energy metering rules restricted renewable-energy generation and prohibited the large-scale export of power from the kind of distributed generators that Fort Irwin would have been.

Bari works with the hand he's dealt. The base has constructed a 1-megawatt concentrated photovoltaic array near the horse stables. (Fort Irwin is home to the Eleventh Armored Cavalry Regiment.) The system uses Fresnel lenses to concentrate the sun's rays by a factor of almost five hundred and, importantly, doesn't require any water to generate power. Ground-level solar closer to the housing and facilities area produces 2 megawatts, with most of that power dedicated to the base's new $211 million super-green hospital. The first Defense Department hospital with a Leadership in Energy and Environmental Design (LEED) platinum certification, the 217,000-square-foot building is net-zero energy use, producing all the energy it needs from solar and other renewables. It is also carbon neutral and completely xeriscaped on its periphery. And it's quite beautiful—the kind of light-filled and peaceful healthcare facility that has been shown to promote rather than hinder recovery.

Bari is currently in the process of bringing in a natural-gas pipeline for a new combined heat and power facility and is in the planning stages for a base-wide microgrid with battery storage. He's also got another rooftop solar project in the works for the housing area. "This power plan is going to make us energy secure by 2022, and that is my number one requirement for the mission," he says. If the 12-megawatt cap is lifted for renewable-energy generation on military installations, Bari will be able meet his energy security goal cleanly.

AN ENERGY-SECURE MILITARY installation that has no water is still a future ghost town, however. Fortunately, Bari has an exuberant deputy waging a battle against water scarcity at Fort Irwin. Colleagues call Chris Woodruff the Water Dude. Sometimes evangelical, sometimes a carnival barker, he is always a high-IQ civil engineer—the guy in honors class who has an answer almost before the end of the question. And, like Bari, he's all about the mission.

Woodruff is the water resources manager in the Directorate of Public Works and steward of the base's three aquifers: Bicycle, Irwin, and Langford all lie within Fort Irwin's boundaries and provide the entirety of potable water for approximately 24,000 people daily. For the most part, the aquifers were filled in the late Pleistocene epoch as Sierra Nevada glaciers began to melt. "We have very old water out here, 14,000-year-old water, that we're pulling out of the ground," says Woodruff. It's had eons to collect pretty much every mineral the desert has on offer.

No one knows the point at which the primordial balance between use and replenishment tipped, but at the current burn rate the life of all three aquifers will expire within sixty years. Already, subsidence at Bicycle Basin is creating potholes and fissures across the dirt landing strip there. It's the Water Dude's mission to extend the life of the aquifers and therefore the base itself.

"We've conducted studies with the US Geological Survey to find other aquifers on post to tap into, but that would be highly expensive. We've got to make the best of what we have for as long as we possibly can. It's an issue of sustainability," Woodruff says in his rapid-fire fashion.

Conservation is the first line of attack in the army's Net Zero Water initiative. When Woodruff arrived at Fort Irwin in 2003, the base was using almost 1 billion gallons annually. He immediately instituted water conservation measures—education, leaky pipe and faucet repair, using recycled water to irrigate, "low-hanging fruit," he says—and has, to date, achieved a 30 to 40 percent reduction. In 2015, the most recent year for which there's data, water use was closer to 720 million gallons. He has Fort Irwin's water-waste hotline programmed into his phone, and called it to complain about a leaky fire hydrant during our tour of the housing units.

A sizable percentage of the water savings on base was the product of negative incentives, Woodruff says. Fort Irwin had historically provided water free of charge to its residential units, but in 2015 the base began "mock," or experimental, water billing to all 2,668 units. If households went over the average use for same-size households, it got a mock water bill. The base saw a 20 to 38 percent reduction in water consumption across its housing units compared to 2014, and the bills weren't even real, yet. The real billing is slated to start in 2018.

From conservation, Woodruff went after water treatment. The base had a plant that used reverse osmosis to purify water laden with high concentrations of arsenic, fluoride, nitrate, and total dissolved solids like silica, but the total dissolved solids in particular blocked the mechanical pores so that the plant was only 50 percent efficient—meaning half the water could not be recovered. When explaining the inefficiency of the old plant, the Water Dude worries I don't understand how utterly, totally, completely unacceptable 50 percent is. "I almost want to plot a white board and go crazy!" he exclaims. I assure him I get it, so he continues.

Woodruff is the force of nature behind Fort Irwin's new water treatment facility, which utilizes electrodialysis reversal and is more than 99 percent efficient—99.6 percent to be exact. "It works like an industrial-size kidney machine" to filter impurities, Woodruff explains, adding that each half percent of water recovered adds six months to the life of aquifers and base. Irwin Water Works—the named coined by Woodruff—will double Fort Irwin's water supply, to 120 years. It took thirteen years to bring on line, but the plant finally began processing water on May 1, 2016. The holdup was always about the money, not the technology, Woodruff says, adding that the last 10 percent of efficiency is 50 percent of the cost of the $100 million plant.

"This is a 100 percent unique plant," and it can treat 6 million gallons of water per day, the Water Dude says effusively. The base uses an average of 2 million gallons a day and up to 5.4 million gallons in the middle of the summer.

Sean McCarthy heads the Division of Drinking Water for the area's Water Resources Control Board and knows both Woodruff and Irwin Water Works well. He was part of the permitting process. McCarthy says that the IWW treats a relatively small amount of water compared to other municipalities in the Mojave/San Bernardino area and those municipalities could not afford the cost of using similar technology for their volume of need. But he added that IWW's technology was the most efficient on the market and just what the base needed. He is impressed that Fort Irwin chose such cutting-edge technology: "A lot of times when we see military bases they try to do—I don't want to say the minimal amount, but they want to do something that they know is going to work, be reliable all the time, and easy to operate. But Fort Irwin is in an area where the water quality just isn't amenable to the easier treatment technologies, and so they looked to these more innovative forms."

At the ribbon-cutting ceremony for Irwin Water Works, Assistant Secretary of the Army for Installations, Energy, and Environment Hammack noted that "the scarcity of clean water is not only an issue here in the state of California, but it is an issue around the world and in many of the areas where our soldiers deploy." The technology is exceedingly pricey at the moment, but the IWW is now among the most advanced water treatment facilities in the army or anywhere in the world. It's setting the bar and hopefully opening the dialogue about how to deploy the technology more broadly.

"We're doing all this stuff not just because the army needs

water, or because the state's dry, but because we're advocating on behalf of the servicemen and -women behind us," Woodruff says. He has driven me up to a water storage tank atop a hill above the Irwin Water Works. The spectacular view takes in the vast desiccated expanse of the base. In the distance, I can see the combat town Ujen and dust being stirred up beyond it by military maneuvers. The Tiefort Mountains loom to the south. Woodruff is right about the treatment facility's benefit to servicemen and women on base now and in the future. But the effort to bring on line Irwin Water Works—and, more broadly, to build a LEED-platinum hospital; avoid spilling toxic chemicals all over the place; and power the installation with solar and any other cutting-edge renewable-energy technologies the Directorate of Public Works can get its hands on is visionary work that benefits all of us. The average Joe may not be able to secure an Energy Savings Performance Contract like the kind that allows federal agencies to see environmental benefits with no up-front capital costs, but when those contracts bear fruit, we will enjoy collateral benefits. What's more, the military's hierarchical and authoritarian structure, which has proven itself capable of wreaking havoc, has shown itself here to be capable of shaping an army of quirky, committed energy innovators and stewards fighting for environmental good. The army's National Training Center at Fort Irwin may be a god-awful rocky desert outpost in the middle of nowhere, but it also turns out to be a hidden green gem.

CHAPTER 2

VOICES FROM THE PAST, PREMONITIONS OF THE FUTURE

NAVAL AIR WEAPONS STATION CHINA LAKE

Presiding over a cache of the Mojave Desert bigger than Rhode Island, as well as 20,000 square miles of restricted air space overhead, Naval Air Weapons Station China Lake is the US Navy's largest single landholding. The "lake" itself is a vast and bone-dry depression that holds water only after heavy rain, which is rare. Its hard-packed expanse is part of the South Range, where electronic-attack systems designed in China Lake's top-secret laboratories are tested and evaluated. The North Range is currently the main testing ground for defensive systems to counter improvised explosive devices. IEDs have been at the deadly center of twenty-first-century asymmetrical warfare in Afghanistan and Iraq, where conflicts have played out between well-armed national military forces and determined insurgents.

The majority of our country's airborne-weapons systems are developed at China Lake, and it's a busy place. During the morning rush hour, its main gate is clogged with mostly civilian scientists, engineers, and administrators headed to work from homes in the adjacent desert town of Ridgecrest. The drivers flash China Lake IDs and are ushered through by armed camouflage-wearing military personnel. I had gone through the visitor vetting process weeks in advance and was vouched for by my public affairs minder in the car ahead of me. Wraparound shades obscure the young guard's eyes but he smiles and says, "Good morning, ma'am," as he waves me past. Regardless of whether it's a courteous marine or a cop checking my ID, the martial air of authority and attendant weaponry tend to make me jumpy. My heart pounds as I drive through the gate and into the place where deadly weapons capable of massive destruction are made.

The station is about 150 miles northeast of Los Angeles and falls in the rain shadow of the Sierra Nevada—meaning that moisture from incoming Pacific storms gets caught and dropped in the mountains—so China Lake enjoys about 360 clear days a year. In technical speak, the station is VMC 99.5 percent of the time—near perfect "visual meteorological conditions" for testing and observing the systems and technologies developed here.

China Lake's mission supports the navy's research and development, testing, and evaluation of next-generation weaponry. But there's more to China Lake than figuring out how to blow things up: The installation hosts and protects some of the most stunning rock art in the world, while its chemists and rocket scientists toil to increase the military's energy independence by creating renewable and much-cleaner-burning aviation fuels. In 2015 alone, China Lake scientists working in the area of sustainable/renewable chemistry and energy were awarded eighteen patents, any of which could become the next disruptive technology—changing our relationship to the environment as profoundly as the military's development of the Internet did for the way we communicate. Remember, an early version of the Internet was designed in a lab sponsored by the Defense Department's Advanced Research Projects Agency in 1969. Called ARPANET, the newfangled communication vehicle was created for and first used as a data-sharing government weapon in the Cold War. ARPANET's evolution sparked the information revolution that changed the world.

The navy took over the lands at China Lake in 1943, a response in large part to the fact that German U-boats had been wreaking havoc along the eastern shore of the United States and in the Gulf of Mexico. The news had been censored and the public was unaware that in the first seven months of 1942 U-boats in these waters killed five thousand seamen and passengers, more than twice the number of people who died at Pearl Harbor. The Department of the Navy knew, however, and was determined to catch up to and surpass Germany's deadly firepower.

To accelerate its research into rocket and torpedo technology, the navy contracted with the California Institute of Technology, already renowned for the work of its scientists, and especially a group known as "The Suicide Squad" for their bold experiments with rocket fuel, which occasionally resulted in classroom fires and explosions. Moving the rocket experiments into the hills behind the suburban Pasadena campus did not help: Residents living nearby complained of huge booms in the middle of the night when something blew up. So the prospect of being able to do R&D and testing in China Lake's wide-open space was a welcome development.

Two years after the Department of the Navy condemned the land for its own use, China Lake had one thousand buildings and a mostly civilian population that had among the nation's highest concentration of doctoral degrees. To attract these high-caliber scientists and engineers to the outer reaches of the Mojave

Desert, China Lake's founding charter ensured intellectual and scientific freedom. It created a management structure that tapped the administration and resources of the military while letting independently minded civilians do the R&D. The labs were, for all intents and purposes, civilian operations supported by the military and with a civilian technical director in control of the program. US military officers and engineers who understood the threats and the matériel needs in the field determined the "what" of weapons development. China Lake's civilian scientists and engineers provided the technical expertise and solved the "how."

The scientists' enthusiasm for their mission was mirrored by the design of the buildings in which they worked. One of the navy's last "themed" installations, China Lake's international-modernist buildings reflected the high-aspiration/high-risk times in which they were built. Military headquarters look vaguely nautical, the symmetrical and elongated lines of its first two floors giving way to a third-floor perch resembling a lighthouse or the crow's nest on a mast. For 360 degrees, the desert spreads out from the windowed perch; it's easy to imagine a beacon of light emitting from it and disappearing into the void of night.

Michelson Laboratory, across the street from HQ, was dedicated at a ceremony in 1948 to a mission and a nation vastly transformed from the one that had existed even five years before. Some of the nonnuclear explosive components of Little Boy, the world's first deployed atomic bomb, were conceived and developed in "Mich Lab's" predecessor building.

The overall design of Mich Lab is a paean to individual ingenuity and initiative: Its main hall is strung with small discrete labs and is so long it attains a vanishing point. Shiny white linoleum floors and fluorescent tubes of light along the hall ceiling

compound the visual sense that it really does go to infinity—
a sense both exhilarating and vertiginous.

In the 1950s, Mich Lab scientists technically solved a tactical
problem: that of moving targets. Traditional missiles could not
adjust after launch for a target's changing coordinates, so scientists developed a built-in "fire-control system" that could continue to calculate the intercept point in space even as the rocket
sped toward its mark. In 1958, a Sidewinder missile developed
at China Lake and delivered to Chinese nationalists downed a
Communist Chinese fighter plane over the Taiwan Strait, making it the first air-to-air guided missile to be successfully used
in combat. The Shrike, another China Lake creation, was the
world's first operational antiradar missile. Released to the US
fleet in 1965, it would become one of the most-fired guided missiles in history. Robert McNamara, secretary of defense under
both John F. Kennedy and Lyndon B. Johnson, noted that 75 percent of all US air-launched weapons used in Vietnam had been
developed at China Lake.

Since the bloody battles in the jungles of Southeast Asia,
large-scale US military involvement has tended toward areas
with crude oil rather than Communist threat. President Jimmy
Carter succinctly stated the American calculus in his 1980 State
of the Union Address: "Let our position be absolutely clear: An
attempt by any outside force to gain control of the Persian Gulf
region will be regarded as an assault on the vital interests of the
United States of America, and such an assault will be repelled
by any means necessary, including military force." The US has
reconfirmed the linkage between Middle East oil and national
security ever since.

Energy independence as it relates to renewable energy has
multiple national security implications: less reliance on foreign

oil and therefore the often-hostile regimes that control it; and less reliance on the energy resources that contribute to climate change, which has been labeled by the US Department of Defense as a "threat multiplier" because of the environmental and population instability it exacerbates.

Scientists at China Lake are today creating renewable energy in the lab. Although the primary motive for the research is to impart a tactical advantage to the American warfighter, the gee-whiz factor produced by its broader applications—and benefits— are about as heady as it gets.

BEN HARVEY, a former competitive swimmer with a Ph.D. in organometallic chemistry from the University of Utah, is a research chemist at Michelson Lab. His work has focused on renewable fuels since 2007. Tall and athletic, Harvey looks kind of like Buster Crabbe, who played Buck Rogers in a series of futuristic space-adventure films and was a top swimmer himself pre-Hollywood. Harvey definitely does not look like a guy who spends long hours hovered over glass beakers and microscopes. Yet, his accomplishments suggest otherwise. In 2015, a paper he published in the American Chemical Society journal *Energy & Fuels*—on renewable diesel and jet biofuels that he and his team had created in his lab—was named the society's Editor's Choice article. *Chemical & Engineering News*, the world's most-read chemical news magazine, highlighted the article as well.

In his lab along Michelson's endless main hall, Harvey wears a white coat as he decodes his academic paper for someone who's never taken a chemistry class. By combining two types of molecules, he explains, he's created a biofuel that dispenses with the nasty sulfur-based compounds of regular diesel and jet

fuel while maintaining the high-density and combustion properties required by their engines. According to Harvey, the den-
sities of his biofuels exceed those of conventional jet and diesel
fuels by up to 13 percent, meaning they could improve the range
of aircraft, ships, and ground vehicles, while also achieving a
reduction in greenhouse gas emissions of up to 70 percent.

He grabs several beakers for color comparison, holding a
muddy one containing conventional jet fuel up to the light. "This
one has hundreds of molecules. I'm not going to let you smell
it. It contains aromatic compounds, sulfur-based compounds;
really, really nasty stuff." That would be the nauseating stuff one
tries not to inhale when near active airport tarmacs, for example.

Harvey controls his molecules and manipulates their structure so that not only are his fuels clean-burning and high-
performing, but they can act as both a diesel and a jet fuel. He
grabs another beaker, proudly raising it as if for a toast. "Our fuel
has quite a bit higher viscosity." Swirling the liquid around the
glass beaker, he adds, "See? Nice legs on it." When he unplugs
the beaker and lets me take a whiff, it smells like candle wax.

Harvey has also created a missile fuel from cedar that smells
just like the tree. Another of his synthetic biofuels, made from
a compound found in flowers that smells like Froot Loops, per-
forms exactly like JP-10, the traditionally synthesized missile
and jet fuel, he says. JP-10 has been important for military applications because of its high density (propulsion power) and low
freezing point. It's been the go-to fuel for the Tomahawk and
other missiles. Harvey has created a fuel that, he says, "isn't
close to JP-10. It's exactly the same fuel but produced from a
biological source."

In the latest chapter of his work, Harvey is collaborating with
biochemists and using the same fermentation process used to

make beer but doing it to make fuel. "We use metabolically engineered yeast. But instead of producing alcohol it produces sesquiterpenes, the fuel molecules we want."

Much of his funding comes from the Defense Department's Strategic Environmental Research and Development Program. According to Harvey, "The goal is green chemistry: Reduce the toxicity of intermediates, use less organic solvents, try and do things with water. We want to outperform petroleum-based fuels." He and his team won the 2016 Project of the Year from the program for their bio-based-fuel breakthroughs.

In 2013, a Cooperative Research and Development Agreement was signed with the private company Allylix to further develop Harvey's biosynthetic fuels through the fermentation process. R&D is known in the investment world as the Valley of Death, where companies wither and die after pouring millions or even billions of dollars into endeavors that don't pan out. Partnerships like the one Harvey's lab had with the San Diego–based company leverages the R&D might of the US government to ease the R&D risks to private companies. Allylix was acquired in 2014 by Evolva, which continues the biofuels R&D.

"We don't commercialize anything and we don't make a profit. We develop the intellectual property and then we work with companies to produce it," Harvey explains. With oil prices hovering around fifty-seven dollars a barrel, Harvey's biofuel is more expensive than the status quo fuel, but as the price of oil rises—due either to a supply crunch or to its price becoming more reflective of its true environmental cost—his biofuels will become more competitive.

Beyond biofuels, Harvey's team is creating composite materials from renewable sources. One patented process utilizes resveratrol, found among other places in the skin of red grapes.

Resveratrol is in vogue these days and sold at places like Costco; it's thought to be an antioxidant that helps the body fight cancer and heart disease. Harvey likes resveratrol's properties for another reason: His lab has figured out how to make a highly concentrated synthetic version of resveratrol that can be fashioned into what's known as thermosetting resin. He holds up a "show-and-tell" prop—a very thin material made from eight plies of carbon fiber and resveratrol thermosetting resin. According to Harvey, the thing is completely flame resistant. "It can take a blowtorch, even though it's organic. It self-extinguishes! Very exciting." The material is half the weight of aluminum but stronger, and it can be used in the manufacture of lighter-weight and therefore more fuel-efficient aircraft.

Harvey's newest endeavor is to create a material from pine resin to replace methylenedianiline. MDA, as it's known, is a nasty molecule in things like polyurethane, epoxy resins, paint, and high-temperature polyimides used in engine ducts; it is carcinogenic and mutagenic, and employee exposure is regulated by OSHA at ten parts per billion over an eight-hour work day. Harvey's material possesses MDA's positive properties but is noncarcinogenic, nonmutagenic, and "so nontoxic you could eat it," he says, adding, "We're really interested in developing nontoxic solutions to performance issues."

When Harvey was asked by a writer for the Defense Department's official blog *Armed with Science* in 2014 where he would go in time and space if he could choose, he first responded that he'd like to see the birth of the universe. "You hear about how chemists like to start fires and have things explode. Well, the Big Bang would be the biggest explosion ever." But then he added that he'd most like to visit the near future: "I'd like to go maybe 100, 200 years in the future and see what happened to Earth,

America, and the other countries of the world. I'd like to see if we're really making a difference right now and how society adapted to some of the problems that we're currently facing."

Harvey's musings about the future lead me to his look-alike, Buck Rogers. The *Flash Gordon* and *Buck Rogers* comic strips and radio serials of the mid-twentieth century celebrated two science-minded adventurers who inhabit the future. Both were conceived and born into a world in which science was specialized and scientists were making profound discoveries—and also one in which the world warred and no one knew what the future would look like, or even if there'd be one. Kind of like ours.

Whereas in *Flash Gordon*, science is powered by optimism and possibility, *Buck Rogers* represents the cautionary tale. In a short movie made for the 1934 World's Fair, for example, Buck is an astronaut—someone qualified in the science end of things—and the commander of Earth's Interplanetary Battle Fleet. He has survived some kind of apocalypse. His is not a world of American triumph against alien insurgents but more dire and intransigently warlike: a dark future of human destruction and loneliness. In this lo-fi sci-fi drama, titled *Buck Rogers in the 25th Century: An Interplanetary Battle with the Tiger Men of Mars*, an intercepted intergalactic map shows a "war arrow" pointing toward Earth. Buck absorbs the implications stoically, then ventures off in his rocket ship to fight the mutant enemy, while trying mightily to avoid their Tesla-coil-like paralysis rays. I marvel at how much special-effects technology has advanced since the movie was made but wonder how near we are to Buck Rogers's future, given how good we humans have become at fouling our nest.

ALTHOUGH A GREAT DEAL of weapons research and development is done in the labs and then tested on the North and South Ranges, the military utilizes only 3.5 percent of China Lake's 1.1 million acres to carry out its mission. Much of the rest of the landholding is a buffer zone against excess noise and weapon mishap, but still many thousands of acres have been set aside for special protection. The China Lake region has been occupied for more than twelve thousand years and contains riches of prehistory, including the largest and arguably most important concentration of rock art in the Americas. The Coso Rock Art District is a National Historic Landmark, and Coso Hot Springs is on the National Register of Historic Places. Protection of these and other treasures from the ancient past located at China Lake falls to the navy, which has won the California Governor's Historic Preservation Award twice for its stewardship work.

"We use what the navy needs to carry out its mission. What we don't use, we conserve. That's not discretionary. It's the law and we don't have an option not to comply. How we do that, though, is an art form," Captain Rich Wiley informs me in our first meeting. He earned his wings as a naval flight officer in 1992 and commanded the weapons station until December 2016. Dressed in a crisp, loose-fitting one-piece flight suit, his hair cut military short and his jaw square, he tells me that even his daughters when given their first tour of the station were sure that all their dad did was lay waste to things. "That couldn't be further from the truth," he says. "The navy needs to carry on its mission, but we also owe something to those who came here before us."

The National Historic Preservation Act of 1966 and the Archaeological Resources Protection Act of 1979 acknowledge the importance of preserving the nation's past and set federal policy for protecting it from rampant development on federal land. Federal agencies including the Department of Defense are required by these laws to take into account the potential effects of their activities on historic and archaeological properties and adhere to certain legal obligations to protect them.

Mike Baskerville has been chief archaeologist and manager of the Cultural Resources Program at China Lake since 2007. It's his job to ensure that China Lake abides by the law, but his depth of knowledge about the installation's history and pre-history and his enthusiasm for protecting all that falls within his area of expertise is likely key to the "art" of China Lake's resource preservation that Captain Wiley was talking about.

As we climb into his truck, Baskerville says he doesn't like sitting behind a desk and much prefers to be in the field. Burly, bearded, and wearing a baseball cap, he tells me right off the bat that he was in the army for five years and got out right after Operation Desert Storm. I ask if he'd been doing archaeology. "No. I *saw* a lot of archaeology but I was a reconnaissance specialist. They told me I had a weird skill set [as an archaeologist] that fit a need they had." He doesn't tell me what that need was but volunteers that he scouted Iraqi terrain for the military.

He pulls the truck to the side of the main dirt road on South Range and surveys the chalky, still expanse of the China Lake playa, conjuring the ice age around fourteen thousand years ago. "When I look out at this landscape, I just see a very busy place." He sees mastodons, mammoths, ground sloths, and bison grazing on the savanna-like grasslands; and marshes that surround the vast but relatively shallow lake, fed by the glacial drainage from Owens Lake to the north.

People related to contemporary Native Americans of Pai-ute and Shoshone descent were the first to come to the basin, which became an important trade center because it contained obsidian—a precious raw material that was used for making tools and hunting weapons. The volcanic black stone was mined from one of four ancient quarries, located in lava beds around China Lake. Artifacts made of China Lake's obsidian have been found throughout the Southwest, Southern California, and on the coastal Channel Islands. Pottery from the Southwest and shells from the Channel Islands have been found at China Lake.

"Obsidian was a commodity of value, so economically it was very profitable to live here," Baskerville says. "You wouldn't use a screwdriver to take off a bolt. Prehistorically, too, the right stone makes the right tool. A brittle stone like obsidian was good for making points because you get a sharp edge, and it's also good for piercing."

The majority of the work done by Baskerville and his team involves "looking at acreage," inventorying the artifacts they find, and evaluating their significance. "We record the site, but we don't pick up and take anything unless we think that it's going to be destroyed or there's a chance it can be collected by somebody else. We do it to comply with the law for future planning and resource management," he says.

One criterion that makes an archaeological site eligible for the National Register of Historic Places is that it has yielded, or is likely to yield, information important in history or prehistory. Baskerville approaches the landscape with this "criterion d" front and center: "We're trying to figure out what is the researching potential of a site, and in order to do that we need to establish chronology," meaning that they must date the site's artifacts. The most accurate scientific way to identify the period in which people lived is through a process called obsidian hydration. When the obsidian is freshly exposed to the atmosphere—as when an ancient toolmaker deftly cracked it with another stone to make a sharp edge—the black volcanic glass takes up water to form a kind of rind different from the rest of the obsidian. The rind's thickness helps determine age.

Along the eastern "shoreline" of China Lake, one well-studied site 350 meters long appears to be remarkably spread out. Baskerville and others speculate that the wide dispersal of artifacts is due to the "drag" effect on them by the receding waters of China Lake over time. Obsidian projectile points and crescents; hardstone gravers for fashioning rock art; hide scrapers made of basalt; mill slabs and the rounded rocks used on them to crush seeds and nuts; and thousands of flakes have all been found there. A nearby site, much smaller, has also been extensively studied and inventoried. The wide variety of tools and debris at these two sites indicates that they were residential bases, places where raw materials were gathered and manufactured into tools and hunting weapons. The repeated use of these sites over time suggests that the marshland habitat provided predictable seasonal subsistence resources that kept people coming back.

According to anthropologist Emma Lou Davis in a 1975 article for the journal *American Antiquity*, China Lake's "exposed archaeology" contains some of the "richest and most varied archaeological information in North America." She wrote that the site provides key insights into patterns of living and moving, and what distinguished men's work from women's work then. Davis, who died in 1988, was an expert on Paleo-Indian archaeology in California deserts; she also designed aircraft during World War II as a side passion. Her excavations at China Lake were among the first to present evidence that Southern California had been inhabited much earlier than previously thought. Baskerville and his team follow in her footsteps.

So far, 25 percent of the China Lake station has been surveyed for cultural resources, and 16,000 archaeological sites have been recorded there. In the state of California, and in coordination with the tribes, a concentration of ten or more flakes—also called debitage, the detritus of toolmaking—within 100 square meters is considered an archaeological site. In some states, two flakes within 10 meters constitutes a site. "If we did that around here, we'd have hundreds of thousands of sites," Baskerville said. He has so far inventoried 5,500 of the sites. A geographic information system (GIS) is used to continuously update a map of all inventoried areas.

When I ask about the giant plywood targets located in creosote scrub between the dirt road we are driving on and the playa just to the west of us, Baskerville explains that weapons testing since the first Gulf War has increasingly focused on accuracy: "We want to make sure we're delivering the ordnance where it needs to be, not where it's skipping around doing what it wants. We test a lot of munitions that, when they're fired from an aircraft, are going to hit the target they are supposed to hit and it's not going to do any more damage than is absolutely necessary."

Good news, I think, as Baskerville fires up his walkie-talkie to call in our coordinates to the range operators overseeing the weapons' tests. Once cleared, he heads east up Mountain Spring Canyon, gaining 3,500 feet as he drives into the Coso Range. He points out a large hill and offers a glimpse into how an archaeologist visually maps the terrain: "It's called Red Hill because the mariposa lily grows there. When the lily blooms the hill turns orangish red, which tells me there might be a prehistoric campsite close by. Mariposa lilies are a food source. At least in this area, Native Americans were matriarchal and women chose the campsites. They gathered and processed the plants, and took care of kids, so they needed to be close to food and water." There were a lot of villages around that hill, he says.

When we reach the plateau about an hour later, the elevation affords a breathtaking view of the playa and the snow-capped Sierra Nevada beyond. Baskerville's conjuring of village life makes it easier to look at the vista and imagine the shallow waters of the prehistoric lake, surrounding marshlands, and wisps of smoke curling upward from the campfires. Daily life and the grind of survival happened in the basin, and around Red Hill. We are headed to where the dreamers dreamed and art was made. The 36,000-acre Coso Rock Art National Historic Landmark is remarkably undisturbed and contains more than 20,000 documented images. Of the landmark's main canyon systems— Big Petroglyph, Little Petroglyph, Sheep, and Upper Renegade— Baskerville chooses Little Petroglyph, a deep wash cut into Wild Horse Mesa and lined with basalt rocks whose water-smoothed surfaces made perfect canvases. Although the area is restricted, US citizens have access to the sites during specific dates in the spring and fall, in limited-size tours organized in coordination with the navy. Contractors working with the navy have nearly completed a 3-D virtual tour of the petroglyphs. "Not everyone can come out here, but they're still interested. Maybe they're from a country where they're not allowed to come on our military bases. We are creating a 3-D tour that's no problem for national security, creates no issues with our mission. So, for instance, researchers from all around the world can put on their 3-D goggles and come down here virtually. They can take the measurements, they can find out the geographic location, they can take a picture of it by pushing a button. We're soon going to be able to share this place with the larger scientific community." Part of the project is already up on the Internet.

Baskerville says it took three weeks to capture the first 200 meters of canyon. "It'll fit with a gaming platform, like Xbox," he says. "We want people to have a good time and discover on their own, so it won't be a 'guided' tour. It'll be just like being in the canyon, except it will be in a climate-controlled environment without bees."

Little Pet, as it's known, contains both petroglyphs (rock engravings) and pictographs (rock paintings). Petroglyphs represent the vast majority of its rock art. A stone cobble harder than basalt was used to hammer through the basalt's surface coating, called desert varnish, to create a design in the lighter rock exposed below. Besides the crunching of our boots in the sandy arroyo, all is quiet. And yet it is not. From the dark volcanic rock a lost language emanates.

There is no consensus among archaeologists or even local Native Americans about who made the rock art or what it means. "People are making this art eight thousand, five thousand, fifteen hundred years ago. We can tell that by the types of weapons: spears, atlatls, bow and arrows," says Baskerville, but little else is clear. Rock-varnish dating techniques have been used at Coso, but Baskerville sticks with the weapons to tell his tales: The spear was first used eight thousand to ten thousand years ago to hunt in this area. The atlatl period came next, from eight thousand to fifteen hundred years ago. "Atlatl" is an ancient and exotic word whose principle is familiar to most modern-day dog owners. The Chuckit! ball launcher is our modern atlatl, exponentially increasing the distance a hand-thrown ball can cover. The atlatl was used to propel ancient darts and spears—depending on the prey—with more deadly power than a hand-thrown weapon alone. The bow and arrow came into use around fifteen hundred years ago. A spear or an arrow, pecked into the basalt, is sometimes lodged in a bighorn sheep. Beyond that, says

Baskerville, we know little more than that the artists' "existence and mythology was entirely different from our own."

To be down in Little Pet Canyon is to be immersed in bighorn sheep, which comprise about half the imagery, as well as intricate humanlike but otherworldly figures called pattern-bodied anthropomorphs, and shapes—circles, spirals, wavy lines, rectangles. Regardless of meaning, one can't help but get an inchoate sense of presence, like the feel of water on skin when floating in a calm sea.

Although I know Baskerville is disinclined to speculate, I ask about a petroglyph visible on a low basalt boulder. By the bow and arrow depicted, he knows it was made fewer than fifteen hundred years ago. The panel appears to show two bowmen shooting at one another. He adds as a side note that the area was not known for warfare. Fluid tribal boundaries among the different groups of original inhabitants, thought to be Coso Shoshone, Kawaiisu, and Northern Paiute, likely contributed to relatively peaceful relations, he says. "Talking to Native Americans in different places around this area, they tell me, 'Yeah, there were times when the piñon nuts didn't grow in the mountains nearby, so they'd have to go farther north. But as long as they checked in with those they came in contact with, and were respectful, and didn't take it all, there wasn't a problem.'" Intermarriage, known to have occurred between members of different groups, likely encouraged comity as well.

Before he died in 2013, Ron Wermuth, a respected and knowledgeable Native American elder affiliated with various tribes of the region, refused, like Baskerville, to speculate about any of the petroglyphs. "I don't try to understand them. I don't know what they *mean*. I can feel them," he told an interviewer shortly before his death. For Wermuth the rock art offered up an invitation to be still and open, not to know but to commune.

Wermuth did, however, have much to say about the naturally occurring geothermal pools that have been used for millennia by Native Americans. The Coso Hot Springs are part of the weapons station. In the documentary film *Talking Stone: Rock Art of the Cosos*, Wermuth noted that, "In Paiute-Shoshone culture, [Coso Hot Springs] is where the beginning of mankind took place. Spirits reside here. The breath of Mother Earth comes up in the steam." He explained how he, his parents, and all those who came before them visited the springs for ceremonies. The mud has transformative properties, Wermuth explained. "The spirits can't see us until we put the mud on our face. It identifies us to them."

In 1909, without permission from the Native Americans who used the area, a "healing resort" was built on the sacred site. Advertising the mud's health-giving powers, the spa promised to cure all types of vexations, from stomach ulcers to arthritis. The resort was out of fashion among Anglos by the 1940s, so few besides local tribe members protested when this ancestral land was again repurposed—this time by the navy as part of what would become its top-secret test site.

In 1978 Coso Hot Springs was added to the National Register of Historic Places for its "aboriginal religious significance," making official what local tribes had known for thousands of years. The designation did not restrict the construction of a geothermal power plant in 1987, however. Admired by many environmentalists for the clean, renewable energy it produces, the Coso Geothermal Field is one of the largest producers of geothermal electricity in the country. Its nine turbines can generate a maximum of 273 megawatts of green, renewable energy, which is sold on to California's power grid under a long-term agreement with Southern California Edison.

The tribes were opposed to the power plant's construction and continue to oppose its operation. In a 2002 Senate hearing on sacred places affected by Defense Department operations, chairperson Rachel Joseph of the Lone Pine Paiute-Shoshone Tribe made her case to the Committee on Indian Affairs. Speaking on behalf of members of her tribe, including her parents, "who have prayed, worshipped, and healed themselves at the Coso Hot Springs," she testified that the mud and water used for millennia by her people had changed, and petitioned the government to restore Coso Hot Springs so that her people "can use the area as they formerly used it, which includes immersing themselves in the water and the mud that was so necessary to [our] healing." Instead, later that year the Department of Energy awarded $4.5 million to several private companies to utilize hydraulic fracturing technology, or "fracking," to enhance the Coso Geothermal Field's productivity.

"Our relationship with Native American tribes is pretty good, except for Coso Geothermal," Baskerville acknowledges. "There, it is not good. It's a conflict point. It's a very important sacred site that's being exploited for geothermal power." The navy has tried to mitigate the problem by allowing Native Americans increased access, he says. "Native Americans have more physical access to all parts of this installation than any other group. If they want to have ceremonies at the hot springs, if they want to take their kids out to a site to talk about their heritage and teach their kids out here, we make that happen." Simultaneous with these efforts, local tribes continue to petition to have the geothermal plant dismantled.

The confluent and paradoxical forces of past, present, and future are powerful at China Lake, more so than any place I've ever visited. China Lake: a stark and beautiful place where the world began and where weapons work could imperil the planet; where the capital benefits of healing geothermal waters flow into utility company coffers, with many environmentalists cheering the clean energy produced by the now desanctified place. But here as well there's space for the human ingenuity of scientists like Ben Harvey, who's working to crack the code on sustainable aviation fuel. It's estimated that each year about eight thousand people die globally from the pollution caused by airplanes. According to researchers at MIT's Department of Aeronautics and Astronautics, the harmful fine particulate matter that wreaks havoc on lungs is created when nitrogen oxides (NOx) and sulfur oxides (SOx)—which make up less than 1 percent of aviation fuel emissions—react with gases that already exist in the atmosphere. Seventy percent of aircraft fuel emissions is carbon dioxide. CO_2 endangers public health and welfare as well, according to the Environmental Protection Agency; it's also a greenhouse gas and significant contributor to climate change. Barring efforts like Harvey's, it's projected that by 2050 aircraft emissions will more than triple to 43 gigatons of carbon dioxide—a dystopian future that even Buck Rogers would be hard put to successfully combat.

CHAPTER 3

MICROGRIDS AND ASYMMETRICAL INFRASTRUCTURE

MARINE CORPS AIR STATION MIRAMAR

When Governor Jerry Brown held the state's highest office the first time in the 1970s, he was a nontraditional leader whose environmental focus went beyond much of the political establishment's. In his second go at the governorship, which ends in 2019, Brown is still out front: He's pushed a climate change agenda for the state that is among the nation's most visionary, and he's led an unofficial group representing states, cities, businesses, and universities to climate talks in Bonn, Germany, where he pledged to abide by the Paris Agreement—even as the Trump administration's official US delegation arrived to promote fossil fuel use.

Brown takes the climate-action fight where it leads him and looks for allies where he can—including the Department of Defense, which is one of California's largest employers. At a meeting with military brass in 2017, Brown thanked them for supporting his climate change initiatives, saying their efforts on military installations around California were making both the state and the military more resilient. Then he asked for more.

Challenging them to jump the ruts of status-quo thinking, Governor Brown said: "We know we have to innovate, and innovation means not doing the same old thing."

The sense of urgency is well founded. In California, climate change is turning up the frequency dial on wildfires, record-breaking temperatures, and extreme weather events; and the California Department of Water Resources warns that climate change is having a "profound" impact on California water resources.

Marine Corps Air Station Miramar didn't need the governor's challenge; it's already ahead of the game and is building what will be the Defense Department's most ambitious and greenest installation-wide microgrid to date. Slated for completion in 2019, the Miramar microgrid will be powered mostly by renewable energy and, at the very least, be able to disconnect, or "island," from the shaky national electrical grid and operate autonomously when necessary. What's more, the air station is building this microgrid while at the same time helping the area quench severe water-scarcity problems. "Energy security" is the buzz phrase these days, but for Miramar it's the energy-and-water-security nexus that matters—a holistic attitude that acknowledges the environmental realities of the region and state. Not bad for a peewee-size air station best known until now as the place where *Top Gun*'s derring-do flight scenes were shot.

At 23,000 acres and constrained on all sides from future expansion by greater San Diego, Miramar is a relatively compact installation. The mission of the Third Marine Aircraft Wing, which is located on the base, is to provide well-trained combat-ready aviation forces capable of short-notice worldwide deployment. Twenty percent of the 9,300 marines and sailors assigned to the air station are deployed at any given time. One recent deployment to Puerto Rico, to deliver 60,000 pounds of food and supplies after Hurricane Maria ravaged the island, occurred just a few days after the air station broke ground on its installation-wide microgrid. Among other things, the microgrid will help Miramar defend against modern contingencies like extreme weather—to name one menace—while also mitigating the installation's contribution to the greenhouse gases known to factor into climate change.

In the quest to ensure a sustainable future for Miramar and therefore its mission, the air station has managed to transform encroachment and proximity to a large urban municipality— downtown San Diego is just 13 miles south—into an asset, venturing beyond the fence line to partner with the City of San Diego on these renewable-energy and water reclamation projects. While the American Society of Civil Engineers gave the nation's energy infrastructure, drinking water system, and wastewater treatment varying degrees of a D grade overall in its 2017 annual Infrastructure Report Card, the Marine Corps and the City of San Diego have embarked on visionary, large-scale public works that break from the underachieving pack. Acknowledging this, in 2017 the US Environmental Protection Agency ranked San Diego eighth in the nation in clean power production. In recognizing Miramar's role in the ranking, the city's assistant director of public utilities, John Helminski, told me that Miramar has been "an excellent partner" to work with.

It's not always easy being Miramar's neighbor. The air station gets a half dozen noise complaints a day about its jets, which fly from 7:30 a.m. until midnight most days. Popular cycling trails that pass through the base have been restricted, and marines have been known to confiscate the bikes of those who don't heed the signs. But the air station's partnership with San Diego is breaking new ground—not just on the infrastructure projects themselves but more broadly by showing how the military can work with communities as a good neighbor to help the region cope with environmental threats.

What is now Marine Corps Air Station Miramar had its roots in the army, which established a National Guard training center on the property in 1917. It became an aviation way station for the navy and Marine Corps in the 1930s. Although Miramar today is home to sixteen flying squadrons and more than two hundred fixed and rotary-wing aircraft, the aviation iteration of the base had a tragic start due to human error and no small amount of technological hubris.

Crossing the Dust Bowl region of West Texas in 1932 from its home base in New Jersey, the USS *Akron*, a helium-filled US Navy rigid airship and the largest ever built, was pummeled by a massive dust storm and forced to stop for repairs at Miramar en route to a scouting assignment in the Pacific. Only nine months before, the *Akron*—also known as the Queen of the Skies—had been christened by first lady Lou Henry Hoover to tremendous fanfare. These were hard times in America and the Great Depression was in full swing. Millions of farmers in the Plains states, displaced by drought and destructive federal agricultural policies, were migrating west toward the promise of California; homeless camps along the route and elsewhere in America were derisively called Hoovervilles; and President Herbert Hoover was about to lose the election to Franklin D. Roosevelt in a landslide. People needed something big and bold to celebrate, and they came out by the thousands for the christening. When Mrs. Hoover pulled the ceremonial cord, a compartment opened in the blimp's belly and a flock of silvery doves flew out.

The *Akron* was two and a half football fields in length and could carry five Curtiss Sparrowhawk fighter planes in its hold. It was new to the world, and certainly to the Miramar ground crew that greeted it when it landed. No one expected or was prepared when the hot California sun caused the airship's helium load to expand. When the airship came unmoored and began to rise, four young sailors tried to hold it to the ground with ropes dangling from its underside. Like Icarus, the men were taken up into the sky. One sailor let go of the rope quickly and only broke an arm in the fall; two hung on too long and died after they lost their grip and plummeted to earth; the fourth was lucky to find a toggle to slip a boot into, and he was able to stand, hugging the rope to his chest for two hours, until crew members on board could reel him in.

By the time the *Akron* crashed into the sea off the East Coast six months later, killing seventy-three of its seventy-six crewmen, Roosevelt was president and his New Deal administration was signing off on massive public works projects to promote economic recovery. Many of those infrastructure projects were designed to last sixty years and are today antiquated, obsolete, and inefficient. A part of that frayed infrastructure is, in short, what the Miramar Energy Project, as it is known, is reimagining. Less hubristic than pragmatically human-scale and collaborative, the air station's contributions to the project are grounded in the realities of technology and cost and driven by a man on a mission.

Mick Wasco had a newly minted undergraduate degree from UC San Diego in structural engineering when he started work at Miramar as an engineering technician in 2010. Two years later he was promoted to energy program manager. His title is somewhat of a misnomer, given that he's the manager of a team of one. As he said when I first met him in 2016, "Energy isn't even a department here; it's just a thing."

Wasco, who has the distracted air of someone with too much to do and too little time to do it, readily admits that luck played a role in his energy innovations. A joint initiative between the Department of Defense and the Department of Energy in 2008 identified ways to reduce energy demand and increase renewable energy use on military installations. As the largest energy consumer in the US government, the Department of Defense had concluded that its use patterns and dependence on nonrenewable fossil fuels were impacting its mission at home and abroad. The Department of Energy then tasked its National Renewable Energy Laboratory (NREL) with devising specific approaches to attaining those goals, and NREL, in turn, chose Miramar as a case study.

When I first reference the lab in conversation with Wasco, I use its acronym but pronounce it NARAL, as in the National Abortion and Reproductive Rights Action League. We were sitting across the table from each other, and when I saw the look of amusement on his face I immediately realized my mistake. I blushed and blurted, "Jeez! That's the abortion rights organization. Not what I meant."

For future reference, NREL is pronounced with the emphasis on the letter N, followed immediately by the first part of "relationship," as in "N-rel." Federal agencies, and the military in particular, employ far too many acronyms as a general rule. But NREL I like because every time I use it now I think about relationships and how things are connected—the matrix of biota, habitats, climates, and basically all of life. If I have a bias with regard to NREL, and I most assuredly do, it is that I consider the lab a sleeper cell in the contemporary political battle for good science, good government, and good stewardship; and it's fighting on the right side. It is the United States' premier research laboratory for renewable energy and energy efficiency but also takes the lead on cost-effective technology development, commercialization, and deployment. In other words, it walks its talk and works with federal agencies to transform the way energy is made and used.

Miramar was chosen as one of NREL's Net Zero Energy on Installations projects. Generally speaking, "net zero" means energy self-sufficiency based both on reduced demand and on use of local renewable-energy resources. NREL's refined definition of net-zero energy for military installations requires that each one "produce as much energy on-site from renewable-energy generation, or through the on-site use of renewable fuels, as it consumes in its buildings, facilities, and fleet vehicles." NREL's net-zero project for military installations does not yet include tactical aviation fuel in its calculations, but if the R&D efforts of people like Ben Harvey at Naval Air Weapons Station China Lake pan out to create high-performing commercially available renewable jet fuel, installation net-zero energy will take on an even more impressive meaning.

As NREL was winding up its analysis of Miramar in 2011, the region-wide electrical-grid failure knocked out power to Miramar and all the other military installations in the area. Training missions stopped at Miramar. "A lot of our security systems were compromised, and marines had to guard ordnance," Wasco said.

"It wasn't theoretical anymore, it was actual," said Sam Booth, senior project leader at NREL and the point person on Miramar, referring to the blackout and its real-world consequences. "A lot of folks were able to see the impacts. It went from, 'Hey, we're going to design you a system and its backup power if the grid goes down, or if there's an attack or something,' to people really understanding the need."

NREL's resulting reports, titled, *Valuing Energy Security* and *Targeting Net Zero Energy at MCAS Miramar*, focused on practical recommendations—many tailor-made for Miramar. Among the most resonant were the steps needed for the air station to be able to delink from the nation's electrical grid and not depend on utility providers to power its mission-critical functions, which include the seamless operation of the hundred or so buildings along the installations flight line next to its airfield.

As Wasco recalls, his initial impetus for reaching toward net zero had been to build renewable on-site energy-generation systems that would be cleaner and cut costs, both worthy goals in their own right. But the power outage "marked the moment of change in energy management" for him. "I'm now realizing that we could use those [renewable-energy] assets to provide us with resiliency and security and mission capability. It's not just something to do to make the bugs and bunnies happy, it's to become more effective at our mission."

Unlike environmental programs, driven as they are by decades of federal law and accompanied by budgets, energy programs like Wasco's are comparatively new. For example, there are approximately twenty employees in Miramar's environmental department. Wasco is a one-man band. The air station secured $20 million from Congress in 2014 for the installation-wide microgrid, but that doesn't cover the rest of Wasco's master plan. He's had to get creative to find additional funding, capitalizing on public-private partnerships; leveraging budget-neutral Energy Savings Performance Contracts that allow federal agencies to upgrade or initiate efficiency and renewable-energy projects with no up-front cost; and using sheer scrappiness to move his energy projects forward. "Mick is a kind of visionary in the Marine Corps," said NREL's Booth. "Having worked with a lot of people in his position across the Department of Defense, Mick has the willingness to be innovative, to work hard, to take risks. He goes above and beyond in a way that a lot of others don't. He wants to push the envelope."

Wasco's first big foray into energy resiliency came in 2012 when he was approached by the Raytheon Company, which had secured funding from the Defense Department's Environmental Security Technology Certification Program, to become a military host site for testing cutting-edge battery technology. The holy grail of power management is batteries. It's one thing to generate power from renewables, but intermittency makes renewables fickle. Reliable and plentiful battery storage could help transform an unreliable source of electricity into one that could radically transform how power is made, who makes it, and how it's distributed. Miramar signed up.

Wasco worked with NREL and Raytheon engineers to design a building-capacity microgrid that could keep electricity flowing by combining renewable energy from the base's 200-kilowatt solar array with battery storage. Primus Power was chosen to supply the storage: a zinc-bromide flow battery that utilized titanium and a unique design that prolonged battery life. "We thought the technology deserved development," says Wasco. "We could have just bought a bunch of car batteries linked together to make it work, but that didn't have the value I see with the DoD's program to test new technologies." The goal of the DoD's environmental security program is to go beyond standard off-the-shelf commercial projects while avoiding woo-woo super wacky ones. According to Booth, the program's "pre-commercial sweet spot is where a project or two has been completed but there's not yet a really big track record and operating history." That's just where the zinc-bromide flow battery fit.

In 2016 Wasco deliberately knocked out power to Miramar's public works building to demonstrate how his mini microgrid could work. "Basically, we simulated an outage. Everybody in the building saw the power go out." Importantly, his building-capacity microgrid was capable of what's called a black start. Imagine that everything is on and working fine and then there's a sudden power outage. You need to be able to restart things and pick up the building's electrical load equal to what it was just before the power was cut, or have a control system in place that can manage and prioritize what comes on line when. That's a black start, and solar generation alone can't do that. You can't just flood the electrical system with solar power. For want of a better word, solar power alone is not "intelligent" enough to know the load requirement and carry that power where it needs to go, which is why a battery and a smart power system are required.

After the black start, the electricity flowed and the lights came on. Impressively, the test achieved 80 percent solar penetration, meaning that 80 percent of the energy used during the exercise came directly from the solar panels to provide for the building's electricity needs and only 20 percent came from the battery. Computers powered up. "A sign of success!" Wasco says. There were also lessons learned. The goal was to be able to "island," meaning that the building could power up and operate independently from the grid. "We wanted to be able to island the building for seventy-two hours—sustain ourselves for multiple days. But in reality, we faced some limitations with the technology."

To be fully operational, the building required 100 kilowatts of electricity. Even though the base had plenty of solar panels, the battery could not accept that power while providing power to the building. In other words, the battery couldn't charge and discharge at the same time. With those constraints, the Primus zinc-bromide flow battery could provide only eight hours of backup power.

THE BASE HAS ADDED photovoltaic arrays on rooftops and carports so it can now generate a total of 1.5 megawatts of power from solar. The second generation of the Primus battery will be part of the installation-wide microgrid as well, thanks to funding from the California Energy Commission. The commission is also funding a $3 million vehicle-to-grid (V2G) lithium-ion fuel-cell demonstration project on base: Three electric cargo vans and three electric pedestrian vans will provide green transportation. When they aren't in demand they will plug into the microgrid to provide power. "I spend a lot of hours trying to figure out how to use other people's money," Wasco says. "I've been getting involved with California state initiatives. When it comes to clean energy, there are so many opportunities it's crazy!"

The biggest power boost for Miramar doesn't come from the sun or from V2G technology, however, but from garbage—which has helped power the air station since 2012. Unlike Fort Irwin, Miramar has a happy story to tell about trash.

The City of San Diego has leased land on air station property for a landfill for more than half a century; today it's at 1,500 acres. One can see the air station's landing field and hangars from the dump. Each year, more than 900,000 tons of trash come through Miramar Landfill's gates. A huge recycling facility is just inside the fence line, but notices and bins along the main dirt road alert drivers that they have another chance to deposit recyclables before they reach the actual tipping point for trash. Along the route there's a turn-off for the Miramar Greenery, where curbside clippings destined for the waste stream have been diverted and transformed into mulch, compost, and wood chips. San Diego residents can drive in and take up to 2 cubic yards of the stuff for free, while landscapers and other commercial outfits pay a nominal fee.

At the active landfill cell, where commercial trucks actually dump the trash, high moveable backstops keep floaty plastic bags from blowing off site, and employees with bright orange vests and hard hats orchestrate the traffic flow. The city runs a tight ship on the air station's land. There's a lot of beeping, the automatic warning that a dump truck is backing up. As soon as trash is dumped, a tricked-out earthmover starts compacting it. By closing time each day, the garbage has either been covered with dirt or a temporary tarp material. The effort keeps down the accumulation of ravens and seagulls, which could get sucked into jet engines and pose a threat. The bird control program is part of the longstanding contract between the city and the Department of the Navy.

Throughout the landfill, one can spy pipes jutting from the ground: The Miramar Energy Project, a joint venture between the air station, the city, and an energy development company, captures methane from the landfill with this pipe system—the pipes act like little vacuums that suck up the methane—and transforms it into energy. Methane—straight out of the ground, produced by decomposing organic landfill waste; or straight out the backsides of livestock, produced as one would imagine—is a potent greenhouse gas. According to the Intergovernmental Panel on Climate Change, while the better-known carbon dioxide (CO_2) persists in the atmosphere for centuries to warm the planet, methane does much worse damage in much shorter time: methane has twenty-eight times the heat-trapping power as CO_2 over a hundred-year period. When methane is captured, refined into natural gas, and burned, however, it enters the atmosphere as CO_2—still a greenhouse gas but far less potent. In a climate-changing world with no silver bullets on the horizon, prettified methane from leaky landfills is a lesser evil compared to coal and other fossil fuels.

Not only did the initial phase of the project drastically reduce the amount of raw methane emissions escaping from the landfill, a refinery and power plant built there currently produces 15 megawatts of renewable energy. Of that amount, 3.2 megawatts go directly to the air station through dedicated infrastructure to supply 37 percent of its average electricity needs. The rest goes to power City of San Diego public works, like its demonstration wastewater reclamation plant, which produces 1 million gallons a day of reclaimed water. The air station satisfies around 30 percent of its water needs by using some of that reclaimed water for landscaping, for street sweeping, and in toilets. Landfill gas also powers San Diego's Metro Biosolids Center, which processes sludge at the landfill.

The Miramar Energy Project is a matrix that excludes the area's investor-owned utility, San Diego Gas & Electric. The City of San Diego contracted with Fortistar to build the landfill power plant and pay for the pipes that run the gas to its facilities, and build other necessary infrastructure as well. The air station has done much the same for its infrastructure. According to one energy expert I spoke to, the fact that the air station and the city's water agency—both historically large consumers of utility-provided power—are finding ways to break free of what has essentially been a regulated monopoly is of great concern to SDG&E. As well it should be: These kinds of changes to business as usual threaten to disrupt the traditional power-generation-and-provision paradigm, opening the possibility of a new energy frontier where those suffering bureaucratic inertia are left in the dust.

The population in San Diego County is one of the fastest growing in the nation and is expected to reach nearly four million by 2050. Not only does that put a stress on the electrical grid, it also increases the demand for water: Currently, the county imports 85 percent of its supply, and costs have grown exponentially. In 2000, water was $400 an acre-foot; by 2016, it was $1,200 and continues to rise, according to San Diego's assistant director of public utilities John Helminski.

Since water conservation efforts began in San Diego in 2007, the city has been able to reduce its water use by 17 percent even as the population has grown. But with population trends ever upward, and Western drought part of the new normal thanks to climate change, in 2014 the city launched the $3 billion Pure Water project to help ensure that San Diego can continue to thrive both economically and environmentally. The air station is part of this project, as Pure Water will be powered by the landfill in its Phase 1 iteration. This is what twenty-first-century sustainability infrastructure looks like, and though the particulars aren't necessarily pretty the sum of the parts is impressive, even elegant. Here's how it will work:

The landfill, which currently captures 50 percent of its methane emissions to provide 15 megawatts of power, will add capacity so that it can capture nearly all the emissions. As part of its installation-wide microgrid project, the air station will get a piece of that action, adding another 1.6 megawatts to what it already utilizes from the landfill. When approached about getting the additional power, "Of course the city said yes," Helminski told me, adding somewhat tongue in cheek, "seeing as how we being good neighbors and they being our leaseholder we are more than willing to do that." The rest of the new landfill power, upwards of an additional 15 megawatts, will provide the electricity needed for the upgrade and expansion of San Diego's North City Water Reclamation Plant just northwest of the air base.

The North City facility was built as a demonstration project in 2011. To date it has performed more than 28,000 water-quality tests on the 1 million gallons of purified (though still non-potable) water it produces each day from—okay, let's just say it—sewage. In the next phase of Pure Water, expected to be completed by 2021, North City will build a LEED-certified advanced water treatment plant across the street, add several additional and critical steps to the treatment process to bring it up to state and federal drinking standards, add additional generation capacity so it can transform the landfill gas into power on site, and produce 30 million gallons per day of high-quality drinking water. When Phase 3 is completed, in 2035, San Diego will be producing 83 million gallons of potable water a day, one-third of its drinking-water demand.

The Pure Water process is complicated and energy intensive—and kind of gross-seeming until one realizes that much of San Diego's pricey and imported water, drawn from the Colorado River and the canal that conveys water from Northern California to San Diego, is also wastewater that has been treated and then put back into the system. Still, the Pure Water concept takes some getting used to. Like I said, it ain't pretty and I admit to balking at first when Helminski offered me a glass of water produced by the advanced five-step treatment process.

(It tasted far better than Los Angeles tap water.) Pure Water is a level-headed yet forward-thinking endeavor that will help the City of San Diego slake its thirst, upgrade its infrastructure, and better control its destiny. Mick Wasco is riding that wave at Miramar.

WHILE WORKING TO BRING the building-capacity microgrid on line, Wasco was simultaneously working with NREL on the installation-wide microgrid project. During peak-load demand, Miramar requires 14 megawatts of electricity to power the base. The average load is 7 megawatts and the minimum is around 5 megawatts. If it works as planned, the installation-wide microgrid will utilize a mix of renewables, battery storage, and diesel and natural gas to generate reliable power on base, ensuring energy security at all mission-critical buildings along the flight line.

"You hear that construction?" Wasco asks as we sit in the public works building. Beyond the wall, sounds of hammering and sawing can be heard. It's been a year since our first meeting and little over a year since the building-capacity microgrid proved itself, and Wasco is finally getting a dedicated energy office and control room as part of the larger installation-wide microgrid. He's obviously pleased, though no less harried.

NREL had run the numbers for the air base; it had calculated costs and taken a deep dive into the relative benefits of using particular energy sources to achieve energy security. According to Wasco, the air station currently uses 40 percent renewable energy—3 percent photovoltaic and 37 percent landfill gas. When the installation-wide microgrid powers up, it will use 60 percent renewables due to the increased power coming from the landfill.

Wasco underscores that, while operating, the microgrid will

likely use a high percentage of renewables, but a certain amount of conventional generation may be required for reliability and surety. Landfill gas, like any other renewable, is not consistent, he says. "Sometimes the quality changes and it causes generators to trip off line." So, in addition to the 1.3 megawatts of solar and the 4.8 megawatts of landfill-gas power, the air station will build a $13 million plant powered by 4 megawatts of diesel and 3 megawatts of refined natural gas supplied by SDG&E. The air station's on-site plant will provide backup when landfill-gas generation lapses, but during low demand almost all energy needs can and will be met by landfill gas and solar, he says.

Wasco, ever the engineer and realist, is resigned to this conventional and renewable mix. "When you have to think about operating your own grid, reliability and power quality are big deals." He's looking to the future as well, though, and turning to his alma mater, UC San Diego, for an assist. They've partnered and are on the trail of another grant from the California Energy Commission, this one to provide funding for battery storage large enough to deal with the inconsistencies inherent in large-scale landfill-gas use. This, in addition to Wasco's other battery storage projects, "would mean we could use it alongside landfill power and mitigate having to use diesel," he says. "The benefit to the state in our grant proposal is that we would not be burning diesel but instead be replacing it with energy storage— assuming that it works. This is another demonstration project! But that's what California wants to invest in," i.e., ways to make dirty fossil fuels obsolete, Wasco says.

Even though Miramar's diesel engines are going to be certified Tier 4, the cleanest technology on the market, the injection of a fossil fuel into Miramar's resiliency plan is a bit of a buzz killer for me, so I ask NREL's Sam Booth if they couldn't have found another way to make the microgrid hum without it. "There are other ways, but they're mostly cost prohibitive. The scale of batteries Miramar would need to ensure power for half the installation just isn't economically feasible. Technically feasible? Sure. No one would do it, but there's no technical reason you couldn't," he tells me.

I ask how long he thinks we will be stuck with a reliance on diesel. "I think about that a lot," he says, explaining that diesel generators are relatively cheap to buy but expensive to run, which makes them the go-to emergency choice when the grid goes down temporarily. "They have resiliency value and cost you less up front," he says. The more expensive (and cleanest) option would be photovoltaic power combined with a battery storage system. Though not cost effective and therefore not realistic yet, such a system "would have grid-connected and resiliency value," Booth says, meaning such a system could conceivably contribute to the region's power needs when those needs are highest, while serving the base's needs at all times.

The important word here is "conceivably." Regardless of whether the power is generated by diesel or clean, green renewables, Miramar and all other military installations in California are currently restricted by law and Public Utilities Commission regulations from exporting excess power back onto the grid. According to Wasco, there is even technology in place at the air station to make sure of this. The installations are also prohibited by the same PUC regulations from being paid for that power, even if they were able to put it on the grid. But what if Miramar were allowed to provide power to the grid when it was really needed, say, during peak electricity demand between 4:00 and 9:00 p.m. daily, and be paid a fair price for it in the form of what's called a feed-in tariff?

Sam Booth isn't the only one thinking about how to harness Miramar's microgrid potential. As the California state director of the US Marine Corps West's Office of Governmental and External Affairs, Ned McKinley's portfolio of duties includes working with lawmakers and others to help make the lives of military personnel in California better. That said, a "big chunk" of his time is taken up with installation energy issues related to cost, reliability, and security, he says. For McKinley, the Miramar microgrid presents a world of possibility that benefits not only the air station but the larger San Diego community as well.

McKinley imagines that Miramar's microgrid could become a pilot demonstration project: with a feed-in tariff, the air station could be incentivized to generate power for the state at peak times to prove its benefit to the surrounding community while also meeting the energy security needs of the Marine Corps. "We are putting in place state-of-the-art technology that produces renewable energy and can interact with the grid for everyone's benefit. That's valuable; that's worth something. If fairly compensated, Miramar could help pay for its microgrid 364 days out of the year by putting power on the grid. And on that one day when fires or something take out multiple transmission lines, the installation would have the ability to hold on to that power and go into island mode and still land and take off aircraft safely." The air station's location makes this idea even more practical, adds McKinley, because "it's right in an urban area near load centers."

It seems such a simple and straightforward idea. Wasco is on board with McKinley's pilot-project notion and in fact had floated a similar scenario when I first met with him. The problem is that one person's proof of concept is another's hit to the bottom line. "Utilities need to come up with a new business model so that they are not an impediment to this interconnected grid of grids," McKinley says. SDG&E had a successful demonstration 4.6-megawatt microgrid project in Borrego Springs, which also utilized a combination of diesel, solar, and battery storage. The company is now working on connecting its microgrid to a nearby 26-megawatt solar field, but there's been no discernible interest yet in allowing military installations to produce and supply power in the way McKinley and Wasco suggest.

Miramar's microgrid is located at the four-way intersection of political will, technical reality, economic feasibility, and aspirational goal, and it therefore reflects the fundamental challenges to the widespread deployment of renewable energy. In California, forward-leaning renewable-energy targets and market-driven green incentives have jump-started a good deal of innovation and technology adoption, while market mechanisms and regulation have worked to disincentivize diesel and natural gas use. Miramar's microgrid could be the next step: Were it able to prove itself useful in achieving energy security for the air station and, at the same time, alleviate stress on the electrical grid and further California's climate-action goals, the state would be that much closer to building its much-needed twenty-first-century sustainable infrastructure. A greener future is dangling right in front of us; it would be a pity to not seize it.

CHAPTER 4

GOOD STATUTES MAKE GOOD STEWARDS

SAN CLEMENTE ISLAND RANGE COMPLEX

From the depths of the ocean floor to 80,000 feet overhead, the San Clemente Island Range Complex is the beating heart of the Pacific Fleet's training area. The land, air, and sea ranges cover more than 2,600 nautical miles just off the coast of Southern California—close enough to the fleet's principle home port of San Diego to make for an easy back-and-forth, yet far enough from population centers to allow for weapons and electronic-systems testing and evaluation. It is the navy's only remaining live-fire ship-to-shore and air-to-ground range; it's also the primary theater for the third and most brutal phase of Basic Underwater Demolition Training. Graduates of this training, which occurs on and around San Clemente Island, become special warfare operators and are well on their way to earning the trident that marks them Navy SEAL (Sea/Air/Land) team members. After the terrorist attacks of September 11, 2001, training tempo on the island increased 25 percent and the Department of Defense built a $21 million realistic facsimile of a US embassy compound to train SEALs and other troops in urban warfare and rescue.

Although strictly off-limits to everyone else, getting to San Clemente Island is a breeze for those with military clearance. Travelers take the twenty-five-minute flight at taxpayer expense from Naval Base Coronado in San Diego to the southernmost of Southern California's eight Channel Islands. The nineteen-seater is full the late-fall morning I fly, with several camouflage-wearing marines looking scrunched and uncomfortable in the tight quarters. I have a window seat and plenty of room, and I'm psyched for the chance to see this restricted-access island.

It's overcast at takeoff, but as we approach San Clemente from the southeast, the fluffy marine layer parts and a dun-colored landscape is suddenly plying the choppy seas. Twenty-one miles long and only four and a half miles wide at its thickest, San Clemente Island is even shaped like a ship. A stiff wind makes for a turbulent approach, but it still strikes me as a sweet way to commute to and from work.

Only 2.3 percent of the island is developed with roads or military facilities, and only about 10 percent of the 275 military and civilian personnel that work on San Clemente Island live there year round. There's a flurry of activity at the small airport when our plane arrives: Cargo is quickly off-loaded, including a shipment of crickets that I'd learn later are fed to captive endangered shrikes; passengers board; and the plane takes off. Beyond the plane engine's noise, there's gunfire in the distance. Tenant commands from the navy, Marine Corps, and other military services are almost constantly engaged, somewhere, in exercises. Gunfire and the concussive thunks of heavy artillery can be heard to the north.

The US navy trains fiercely in the island range complex to make the world safer for Americans. Those efforts have not had salutary effects on some of the other inhabitants here—

especially the whales. No dive into the navy's environmental stewardship record can avoid the watery depths off San Clemente Island—in which migrate or dwell the majestic blue whale, the largest animal ever to have lived on Earth, along with beaked whales and other threatened and endangered marine mammals. The mammals' human advocates—in particular lawyers for the Natural Resources Defense Council—have argued since the 1990s that the navy's unchecked use of sonar here violates environmental law. By every substantive legal measure on the merits of the claims, the courts have agreed with the environmentalists.

If anything constrains the firepower of the US military on San Clemente Island and its environs it's these and other threatened and endangered flora and fauna—and the visionary federal laws enacted to protect them. The National Environmental Policy Act of 1970, the Marine Mammal Protection Act of 1972, and the Endangered Species Act of 1973 are all sharply crafted prongs on a kind of green trident—prodding the navy to do right by the twenty-one terrestrial or marine federally listed species and other living things that call the San Clemente Island Range Complex home.

All three of these landmark environmental laws were either cosponsored or championed in Congress by Californian Pete McCloskey, a decorated veteran and idiosyncratic Republican who loves his state's natural beauty and wanted to ensure it would be there for future generations. His efforts of almost half a century ago continue to be a work in progress, and will be as long as the laws stand. In fundamental ways, San Clemente Island can be seen as a living laboratory for the legislation. Its isolation offers a window into how discrete ecosystems (and their human stewards) respond to environmental impact, environmental law, and environmental redress.

The navy has sometimes led the conservation charge, sometimes lagged until prodded into action with that green trident of law. The net effect of its efforts, however, has been important new science, a deepening understanding of how ecosystems work, and the chance for threatened and endangered species not just to survive but to thrive in the complex.

WHEN PRESIDENT FRANKLIN D. ROOSEVELT signed the executive order transferring ownership of San Clemente Island from the Department of Commerce to the Department of the Navy in 1934, Adolf Hitler had just declared himself Führer in Germany. The Nazi Party was on the march and holding increasingly well-attended rallies in Germany, where Nazi pamphlets and newspapers full of fake news were distributed to cheering crowds. Hitler was also utilizing a new technology, the phonograph—that era's Twitter—to make recordings of his speeches available to the masses. Roosevelt saw the storm clouds of fascism darkening and knew the United States needed to be prepared to act.

December 7, 1941, started like any other day for Pete McCloskey, an athletic, happy-go-lucky high school freshman in South Pasadena. But when news of Pearl Harbor reached him he was shaken. McCloskey wouldn't be old enough to enlist until after his senior year, but he followed the war closely, especially its heroes. He was particularly drawn to the carrier pilots flying the battles of Midway and the Coral Sea—many of whom trained in and around San Clemente Island.

McCloskey enlisted in the naval air force to be a carrier pilot in 1945. Two months later the United States dropped atomic bombs on Hiroshima and Nagasaki, ending the war. He stayed in the service for eighteen months, then rode the GI Bill to Stanford University undergraduate and law school, where one of his debate partners was John Ehrlichman. Both would eventually choose to practice environmental law and then get into politics. They stayed in touch.

Immediately after law school, McCloskey reenlisted, with the assurance that he'd become a second lieutenant in the Marine Corps. He attended Platoon Leaders Class and then found himself on a ship headed to Korea. At ninety, McCloskey still uses the salty language of his youth to describe his wartime experience. He's not mellowed one bit from being the brash lawmaker who drove his colleagues—not to mention the president of the United States—nuts.

"I get in a rifle company in Korea. I was scared all the time. I knew I was no war hero, but the Marine Corps is a funny deal. You don't want other marines to see you're scared. We were pinned down. We came under machine gun fire....The Marine Corps was a great test for a young man to prove to himself that he wasn't an asshole. Sorry. A coward."

McCloskey was awarded the Navy Cross, the Silver Star, and two Purple Hearts for his actions in Korea. In 1967, after a successful stint in environmental law, he was elected to Congress, where he served eight consecutive terms as a Republican representative, first from Northern California's Eleventh District, then the Seventeenth, and finally the Twelfth.

McCloskey remembers that there were few to zero members of the House of Representatives who were environmentalists when he started out in the 1960s. But he'd spent his life enjoying his state's natural wonders and was listening to constituents who were concerned about emerging environmental threats like pesticides, species decline, smog, and unchecked development.

"Hell, I'd come to Northern California and then run for Congress because I was dedicated to keep from happening up north what had happened in Southern California," McCloskey says. So, he was intrigued when he got a call from the Democratic senator from Wisconsin, Gaylord Nelson, in January 1970.

"He had the idea for Earth Day," McCloskey recounts one day at Rumsey Farm, between Sacramento and San Francisco, where he lives with his wife and five dogs, ten horses, two pigs, three cockatiels, and a crippled goat. "Gaylord said he'd been having cocktails in a friend's home overlooking the Golden Gate Bridge in San Francisco. The sun was setting, it was so beautiful, and someone says, 'We ought to have an Earth Day, like Arbor Day, but it should be something Congress does in a bipartisan and bicameral way.' Someone asks, 'Do you know any environmentalists in the House, Gaylord?' and he says, 'Hell no. I don't think there are any.' Someone else apparently pipes up and says, 'I've heard there's one, some lawyer from out here.'"

McCloskey agreed to be the Republican cochair of Earth Day. Then Nelson's group hired Denis Hayes, a student at Harvard's Kennedy School of Government, to organize university campuses. They set the date for April 22, and in advance sent out information bulletins every two weeks: on ocean pollution, air pollution, whales, animals, land swaps, urban sprawl. "By god, the thing caught fire," McCloskey recalls. Estimates for participation in that first Earth Day are upward of twenty million.

Five days after the event, McCloskey's old Stanford Law School debate partner gave him a call. John Ehrlichman was now an assistant to the president for domestic policy under President Richard Nixon. "John's laughing. He tells me that Nixon was so paranoid about Earth Day observances across the country that he had J. Edgar Hoover's FBI put them under surveillance." (FBI documents chronicling the surveillance were released to the public by Senator Nelson and Senator Edmund Muskie in 1971.)

Earth Day was just the beginning of Nixon's environmental headaches. The celebration's young leaders, stoked by their unexpected success, jumped into the political fray, identified twelve members of the House of Representatives as the Dirty Dozen, and vowed their defeat in the upcoming election. Seven of the twelve, all incumbents, lost their seats in the 1970 election. A new crop was targeted in 1974 and eight of the twelve were defeated.

"Kids changed the course of history," says McCloskey. "Incumbents didn't lose back then. Within twenty-four hours of that [1970] election, I'm getting calls from fellow congressmen who hated my guts, or certainly had nothing in common with me. 'Pete, can we get information on air pollution?' Suddenly people want to understand the issues. Everybody is now an environmentalist! We had a Democratic Congress, and a Republican president that didn't know the environment from a hole in the head. But John Ehrlichman did."

He continues: "By that time I'd studied it and had come out against the Vietnam War. [Because of that stand] I couldn't get on any powerful committees, so I got on a screwy little subcommittee on the Fish and Wildlife Committee. John Dingell [D-Mich.] was chairman, and he and I took to each other. We passed out the National Environmental Policy Act (NEPA) from our subcommittee. We passed out the Marine Mammal Protection Act. The Endangered Species Act, which John Dingell and I cosponsored. All golden environmental legislation."

With the stroke of President Nixon's signing pen, the legislation changed the survival calculus for hundreds of species of plants, birds, invertebrates, and other animals. Department of Defense lands were already guided by the 1960 Sikes Act, which directed the secretary of defense to carry out conservation and rehabilitation programs. But the Sikes Act focused mostly on managing fish and game for recreationists, and collecting fees for hunting and fishing permits. More problematic, under the Sikes Act natural resources protections were discretionary and almost always took a backseat to military operations. The Sikes Act Improvement Act of 1997 broadened the scope of military natural resource programs by integrating those programs with operations and training, embracing the tenets of conservation biology, inviting public review, and strengthening funding for conservation activities on military lands. Importantly, the act required the development and implementation of Integrated Natural Resources Management Plans (INRMPs) for relevant installations.

Yet it was McCloskey's batch of 1970s-era environmental legislation that first laid down the marker for species protection. The National Environmental Policy Act, for example, does not subsume natural security under national security. To the consternation of many (then and now), there is no National Defense Exemption in NEPA. Without frills or loopholes, the law required that federal agencies assess the environmental impacts of their proposed actions and then offer alternatives if called for. (Although the original did not have loopholes, Congress added one for oil and gas in 2005.) The Marine Mammal Protection Act, introduced in response to concerns about significant human-caused declines in some species, is among the earliest federal animal rights legislation in the United States.

The mother of all environmental law, however, is the one that enshrines the protection of threatened and endangered species, and Pete McCloskey knows it. "In all my years in Congress," he says with emotion, "the thing I am most proud of is the Endangered Species Act."

Although the secretary of defense is authorized to specify exemptions from the ESA for reasons of national security, this law has real enforcement teeth. For example, if the US Fish and Wildlife Service, using the best available scientific information, determines that a native plant or animal should be federally listed as threatened or endangered, the imperiled species as well as the ecosystem upon which it depends gains protected status. This status then triggers the requirement that the federal agency overseeing that species and territory develop and implement a recovery plan in coordination with the Fish and Wildlife Service to restore the species to ecological health.

On San Clemente Island, four plant species, two bird species, and one lizard species made the endangered species list in 1977. In fact, it was the only land area on that list with the dubious distinction of having both plants and animals listed. Under the terms of the act, the navy was required to recover and conserve those species and the habitat critical to their continued existence. By then, two island plant species had already become extinct due to habitat loss.

Jan Larsen was a tall, lanky, and athletic biologist fresh from San Diego State University when he was hired in the summer of 1972 to be the San Clemente Island Range Complex's first natural resources manager. He was among the first wildlife biologists hired by the navy, period.

"Being outdoors was natural for me," says Larsen, who retired in 2007 after thirty-five years working on San Clemente Island.

He recalls that when the opportunity arose to talk to the navy about developing a natural resource management program for the island, he lobbied hard for the job. To his surprise, he got it. "I was definitely more book smart than experienced," he now says.

In college, he'd taken a course on the National Environmental Policy Act. As cursory as his knowledge was, fairly quickly he realized that he knew more than his new navy bosses about NEPA. "Let's just say that the navy was just getting acclimated to all the new legislation. Most of the bosses I worked for had to be educated about what the navy's responsibilities were under federal law."

Larsen had been somewhat naive about the navy's overall enthusiasm for his work, but in those early days he benefitted from a few insider advocates. "I had some very forward-thinking military bosses that gave me a lot of free rein. I have to imagine that there were some days when they asked, 'Am I doing the right thing by even having this guy here?' We were strange bedfellows, and we had to work through classic relationship issues. It was an arranged marriage and we had to make it work." That said, he adds, "There was hate and discontent for months, if not years," as he tried to abide by the new laws.

To bolster his conservation arguments Larsen needed to be armed with facts, so he undertook the development of a biological assessment program, or inventory, to determine what kind of resources the island had. He spent his first summer walking it end to end. "A picture keeps flashing in my mind when I think about those first days. A small herd of goats is running away. All you see are their hind ends, a lot of dirt, a lot of rocks, and *no* vegetation. It was desolate." Maps from around that time show hand-drawn shrubs. There were so few that each scrawny plant got its own illustration.

Each year since the installation's founding, tenant commands have fired vast amounts of ordnance onto the island. But according to Larsen, the greatest environmental impact has not been caused by the ordnance, or the noise, or the accidental killing of listed species during training, or even the unintended range fires sparked by land-deployed artillery and bombs. The problem has been the San Clemente Island goat.

Historians date the goat's introduction to around 1875, though no one has been definitively fingered for the epic environmental "don't." When the first official lease was granted by the Department of Commerce, in 1900, to the San Clemente Wool Company for ranching, the island was already overrun by feral goats. Over the course of a hundred years, they continued to multiply into the thousands and moved like an invading army to wreak havoc across the island. Intact and thriving habitats were mown down by what one observer has called "voracious modifiers and destroyers of indigenous vegetation."

For millennia, San Clemente Island had maintained a delicately balanced ecosystem. Between June and August, essentially the only moisture comes from marine-layer fog. Like tiny sails capturing wind, tree and shrub leaves across the island collected mist that gathered into drops that then fell to irrigate the understory. Native grasses grew, shrubs and trees flourished, and the resulting thicket attracted insects, lizards, and rodents—and so also their predators. Depending on soil type and topology, different flora and microclimates dominated. For example, in the dense and sharp confusion of boxthorn habitat the San Clemente Island Bell's sparrow used the spiny plant for nesting and protection. In the more sparse sage scrub habitat, with swatches of open grassland good for hunting between the shrubberies, the San Clemente Island loggerhead shrike thrived.

Radiocarbon samples discovered in the diggings of a military foxhole indicate that there had been visitors and perhaps even settlements on the island ten thousand years ago. But it wasn't until the plague of goats that the island's ecological balance was violently thrown off.

With the disappearance of the plants, there was nothing to capture the fog—a devastating situation for an island that has no natural springs and that receives only about 5 inches of rain on average per year. A negative feedback loop cascaded down the chain of biotic life on the island, which then allowed invasive species to take root. Exotic annual grasses flourished because they germinate and run through their life cycle in a month or two. The life cycle of the native perennial grasses is much longer, and so they were unable to spread seeds before being devoured.

Larsen was all about the goats—numbering between twelve thousand and fifteen thousand by his count upon his arrival. The biological assessment he conducted surmised that they were 98 percent of the island's ecosystem problem. "Between 1934 and when I arrived in 1972, there had been no attempt to contain the goats. The island was a total wreck." Based on the information he collected, a plan was written with the goal of reestablishing, as far as possible, the island's native ecological conditions. He hired three additional scientists to look closely at the plants and animals, "knowing full well that goat removal was tops on the list."

He and his team tried everything: trapping, netting, shooting. They even utilized a "Judas" goat—a radio-collared female goat that led trackers to hidden herds. After the Fund for Animals sued to stop the killing, goats were caught and airlifted off the island for adoption. Whatever was tried, the remaining animals responded to their depopulation by upping their birthrate.

Lethal removal was finally reinstituted, but eradication took two decades: By the time the last San Clemente Island goat departed San Clemente Island in 1991, more than thirty thousand had been dispatched in one manner or another.

Learning how to revivify a land laid waste by unchecked ungulates may seem odd work—a distraction—for the US military, but it's closer to the work of national security and nation-building than one might think. China Lake's head archaeologist, Mike Baskerville, offered a primer on how to destabilize a country when he talked about his tour as a reconnaissance specialist in Iraq: "Iraq isn't a desert for lack of water. It doesn't [lack] agriculture for lack of water. It has water going all over the place. It's just that the soil was killed by ten thousand years of overgrazing, which in turn led to the collapse of what really was one of the first civilizations. People in the US don't really think about desertification all that much, but we need to think about it quite seriously," he told me.

With the goats gone the recovery work could finally start, Larsen thought. But then reality set in. As he was among the navy's earliest biology hires, he suffered from his employer's steep learning curve: "Somewhere along the line, it became patently obvious to me that my role wasn't simply to make an island paradise, with all the wonderful species chirping each morning, enjoying the sunshine as they climb through the sky. My role was to facilitate navy operations."

Larsen continues: "The Marine Corps has this saying, 'We train as we fight.' I needed to conserve our endangered species in such a way that the populations would recover, while also looking at naval operational programs in a way that we could give them alternatives to accomplish their mission that wouldn't adversely affect those populations."

Larsen did not have the power to impel the navy to abide by the environmental statutes. That power fell to the US Fish and Wildlife Service, and Larsen credits the agency for helping him do his job by holding his feet to the fire and mandating he do what he wanted to do anyway. "The legal framework—the federal mandates under the Endangered Species Act, et cetera—drove our natural resources work. But I should also add that our successes were helping the naval operational community understand how we could meet those stipulations and their training objectives. It was a rocky road, but once we gained the navy's trust, and they saw that we would actually help them train as they fight, we got much better cooperation."

The San Clemente Island loggerhead shrike, a subspecies of the widely distributed loggerhead shrike, was Larsen's top priority. By 1998, its population had been reduced to fourteen individual birds in all of creation. He implemented a multiprong program that included habitat recovery as well as the subspecies' first ever captive-breeding program, developed in coordination with the San Diego Zoo. "Just coming up with a diet for the captive population was a *major* issue," recalls Larsen. "One year we had almost no reproduction in the captive flock and it all came back to the fact that we weren't feeding them right. In those early stages, we learned as much from our failures as we did our successes."

But with only fourteen birds left, the margin of error was razor thin and time was of the essence. Environmental groups worried that Larsen's slow progress was going to send the species into oblivion before it even had a chance. In the late 1990s, the Environmental Defense Fund and the American Bird Conservatory threatened a lawsuit if the birds' odds didn't improve. David Wilcove is today a professor of ecology and evolutionary biology at Princeton, but back then he was working for the Environmental Defense Fund. According to him, the lawsuit threat succeeded in accelerating habitat restoration, predator control, and the upgrading of the captive-breeding facilities.

Larsen doesn't remember whether it was the legal threat or his staff's proactive efforts that did the trick, but he does remember that his team continued to work hard and make gains. They changed the cage sizes so the birds could develop flight muscles. They began to feed the birds food they'd recognize in the wild. "People just don't realize that biology is not an exact science. It's not easy to just go out and test things and come back with solid answers six months later. Sometimes you don't see the results, especially in populations, for years. It's really challenging. But my feeling is that if the environmental community is yelling at you from one side and the naval operations people are yelling at you from the other, and you're getting yelled at equally, then you're doing the best job you can."

ALONG WITH CAREFUL HUSBANDRY, habitat restoration has been key to the overall recovery of the island's threatened and endangered species. The navy's botanical restoration program has included the construction of a greenhouse and nursery as well as a seed collection and processing facility. About thirty out-planting sites promote the restoration of habitat for federally listed species. "We've created habitat for shrikes and Bell's sparrows and the island night lizard," says Bryan Munson, who has worked as a botanist on the island since 2010. I meet him on his day off; he's just come from a jog and he's wearing those weird Vibram soled running slippers with toes, which detracts from his obvious expertise. He notes that the lizard, found only on the Channel Islands, had been listed as a threatened species since 1977 under the Endangered Species Act but was delisted in 2014 because its population had rebounded so well.

The removal of the goats was "the best restoration project natural resource managers could have ever done," Munson says in a hat tip to Larsen. Once the goats were gone the remaining shrubs began to proliferate from where they perched, which was almost exclusively on canyon ledges and cliff faces. Invasive species control—including herbicide application and the hand-pulling of exotic grasses, mustard, and fennel—has helped shrubs, boxthorn, and other important habitats recover. Mapped terrain that once showed only a few dozen hand-drawn shrubs today explodes with "millions of shrub plants," Munson says. I don't know what it looked like before, but the northern part of the island I see is rich in swaths of native vegetation.

On the island's west side, time and wave action have carved marine terraces that slope gently from about 450 feet above sea level into the submerged depths of the Pacific. The terraces closest to sea level have a soil and microclimate disposition favorable for the boxthorn habitat critical for the adult San Clemente Island Bell's sparrow, a dainty little bird of 5 or 6 inches with a dark spot on its light-brown chest and what looks like white eyeliner, which gives it a bit of flair. Boxthorn, or *Lycium*, is a genus of flowering plants in the nightshade family. It has tiny succulent leaves and tangles of branches with prickly thorns that make for protective nesting habitat. When ornithologists first sighted the San Clemente Island Bell's sparrow around 1900, it was a common island resident. By the time the goat eradication program began in earnest, the sparrow's habitat had been destroyed and the bird's numbers had plummeted. Its lowest population survey was recorded in 1984 at thirty-eight birds. When habitat began to recover, so did species. As of 2017, thirteen thousand Bell's sparrows were counted on the island, and they have expanded beyond boxthorn habitat.

Munson and his staff are mandated by federal regulation to monitor and maintain restoration sites for five years, but they usually continue the efforts because things don't get interesting until five years in, Munson says. "Very few plants produce or germinate seedlings in the first five years. It's only later that we have significant seedling production. We are going through a very slow process of recovery here, but it is happening across most of the island." Munson notes that the north end gets the least amount of rain, has poorer soil, and is most heavily populated, so restoration is happening more slowly there. "The farther south you go you get nicer soils and more water, and so the recovery is speeding up farther south." Today, San Clemente Island has some of the nicest native grasslands in the entire state of California, as well as boxthorn habitat, he says. "We're doing a lot of good restoration work, but we can't possibly keep up with the natural rate of recovery" now that the goats are gone, Munson says.

The island's unique ecosystem is home to certain subspecies, like the San Clemente Island Bell's sparrow, that exist nowhere else. Few will ever get the chance to see this bird—though the species itself is stable and ranges widely in California and Baja— or the island that's coming back to life thanks to restoration efforts. Under the circumstances, it's fair to ask whether all this work, the biotic fruits of which are mostly hidden, is worth it. But species and habitat preservation isn't a one-off deal; what's learned on San Clemente Island is more broadly relevant to similar habitats and threats elsewhere.

Around the time Larsen retired, Melissa Booker came on board the wildlife biology team to lead the shrike effort. Wiry and solidly built, with thick blond hair she pulls back in a pony-tail, Booker looks the part of a laid-back Southern Californian but describes herself as "Type A," telling me that after she married a veteran navy SEAL who trained aspiring SEALs on the island's north end, it was not she but her husband who wanted to be the stay-at-home parent. Booker was eager to get back to the field and returned six weeks postpartum—"something I wouldn't necessarily recommend." She adds, "When my newborn was sleeping I took the opportunity not to sleep myself but to clean the house." She notes that a San Clemente Island loggerhead shrike had been named after her. "It's called the Shrike Melissa. It killed its mate," she says with a laugh.

They may be endangered, and people may be working diligently to protect them, but it turns out that the San Clemente Island loggerhead shrike isn't a very nice bird. It has a gray head with a black band across its eyes that makes it look vaguely criminal, and the look suits. "They must be housed individually," Booker says as one flits back and forth in its spacious cage. That was one of the primary lessons learned after the first, failed captive-breeding efforts in the 1990s, she says. "Shrikes are aggressive. They do not tolerate each other during the nonbreeding season. They have a very sharp bill called a tomial tooth, and if you keep the pair together one will kill the other. When we do our breeding now, we put two smaller cages side by side that contain a male and a female. You have to see if he's going to feed her and if she's going to accept the food. You put them side by side and see if she does a 'beg display'—their version of courtship. We need to monitor them and make sure they are good."

Another of the shrike's less-than-endearing qualities is that, lacking the talons of a raptor but possessing the raptor's killer instincts for rodents, lizards, and other birds, the shrike catches the prey in its beak and then impales it on the handiest sharp object so it can eat at its leisure. The San Clemente Island loggerhead shrike's scientific name is *Lanius ludovicianus mearnsi,* and in Latin, "lanius" means butcher. They are songbirds that act like ravenous beasts. When we tour the captive-breeding facility, Booker is a little disappointed that techs had been through and cleaned the cages of impaled carcasses; I am not.

Other lessons learned about the birds from the failures of the 1990s relate to the timing of the releases; the manner of rearing, from "hand" to "parent" rearing; and the location into which the birds are released. Booker explains that juveniles are now released into the wild at sixty days. "They survive the best in the wild, so now we get an entire clutch into the wild without losing the adult breeders." She describes another innovation as the modern family approach: "We use adults that can't produce viable eggs anymore but are good parents." They're put in a cage in the wild and lay eggs, but those nonviable eggs are then replaced with viable eggs from within the captive-breeding enclosure. The young pair in the enclosure remain in captivity and continue to reproduce, while the older pair nest on and hatch the viable eggs, feed the nestlings like crazy, and are then released into the wild. "We know those adults probably aren't going to survive, but they're not as valuable to us because they're not fertile anymore. However, they've gotten this clutch of kids off from a pair that's still sitting inside and reproducing."

The genetic lines of shrikes on San Clemente Island have been given whimsical names like Hawaii, Horse, and Metal, with birds named Big Kahuna, Man of War, and Chrome. Chrome has siblings named Bumper and Toaster, et cetera. You get the picture. Then there is the line that produced Trampas—the result of a sister-and-brother pairing.

Trampas had siblings with names like Billy Bob and Brandine. He was exceedingly prolific and perhaps subspecies-saving. By the time he died in 2014, he'd helped make 82 chicks and 782 descendants. Trampas was smart. When he was released into the wild he returned to the area near the captive-breeding facility and hung around where crickets and other insects were off-loaded for feed. He was there to devour any escapees. "He was with Mrs. Trampas for many, many years before she got attacked and killed by a rat," Booker reports. "And then he mated with a first-year female, and then another first-year female. I can't explain why, but Trampas was a stud."

San Clemente Island went from a low of only seven pairs of birds in the wild in 1998 to a high of eighty-two pairs in 2009. In 2013, Booker's natural resources program was honored by the Defense Department for its conservation work: Citing "aggressive and comprehensive recovery efforts" and population increases for the island's loggerhead shrike, as well as increases of all six of the island's listed plant species, the program was highlighted in the award to Naval Base Coronado for natural resources conservation.

In 2002, the San Clemente Island loggerhead shrike became the poster bird in Congress for conservation run amok. During a meeting of the House's military readiness subcommittee in the run-up to the Iraq War, Chair Joel Hefley (R-Colo.) complained that compliance with environmental laws was leading to ever-increasing limitations on training exercises. He reported that, each year, the navy "is forced to close its shore bombardment range off the coast at San Clemente Island—four days each week during the breeding season—due to the presence of a bird called the loggerhead shrike." I ask Booker what she thinks about Hefley's critique.

"We have come a long way from 2002," she replies. "In 2008 we went through formal consultation with the US Fish and Wildlife Service that removed a lot of the encumbrances on the mission out here, on the training, because of the success we'd seen in the shrike program. So what were perceived as limitations on training in 2002 have effectively all been eliminated. Now, the guys who train don't have to think about shrikes. They don't have to know where nests sites are. It's not necessary. We've never had take of a shrike directly associated with operations in any event."

That's not to say the bird hasn't been a burden: To date, the navy's shrike recovery efforts have cost over $40 million. I ask Booker whether the shrike's survival is worth all that money. Her answer surprises me, and underscores the complexity of species recovery and resiliency in an age when man-made threats include the weather.

"I manage the program, so obviously I feel it's important. I am passionate about it," she says, adding that if I'd asked her the same question two or three years ago she would have absolutely made a case that "we can save things." She goes on to say, "But I have watched the shrike population. It has been an incredibly successful program of captive breeding, release, and management, but the population numbers in the wild dropped [in 2015] because of drought. That's the only thing that we can see in the data. So, if you assume that droughts will become more frequent and potentially more intense, which we don't know for sure, but if we assume that that's possible under a climate change scenario...when looking at the Endangered Species Act you have to think about how much is being spent on certain species or certain subspecies and whether or not you know what the chances of recovery are."

One can only hope that if and when this hard look is taken, it is taken by objective scientists with not only specific subject matter expertise but an ecosystem sensibility that weighs the cascading effects of consigning a species to oblivion.

THOUGH THE SHRIKE suffers from a nasty disposition and is definitely not on the list of charismatic fauna, the endangered and threatened mammals offshore have an army of defenders ready to go to court on their behalf.

The legal wrangling over the navy's use of potentially harmful underwater noise began in 1994, when it failed to prepare proper environmental documentation for training exercises that involved blowing up and sinking with torpedoes a ship off the Southern California coast. When the Natural Resources Defense Council got wind of the plans, its attorneys went to court demanding studies that addressed impacts and alternatives. NRDC won that court fight and then began more closely scrutinizing navy activities offshore. Unhappy with the increased oversight, the navy lobbied Congress to weaken the Marine Mammal Protection Act, and in 2004 it succeeded. The National Defense Authorization Act passed that year with an amendment that changed the act's definition of "harassment" to favor the navy.

Research has shown that the loud noises emitted via mid-frequency active sonar has adverse effects on marine life, particularly whales, and could result in permanent injury and even death. So when, in 2007, the navy authorized two years of major exercises off the coast of Southern California that included the extensive use of sonar to locate submerged submarines, NRDC and other environmental groups sued the navy again. In part, they argued that although the navy had prepared an environmental assessment as required under the National Environmental Policy Act, it should have prepared the more detailed and stringent environmental impact statement as required under the Endangered Species Act. The navy countered that it didn't need to go through the added hassle because its assessment had concluded with a "finding of no significant impact"— even though that same assessment showed a take of over 170,000 marine mammals over the two-year course of the exercises.

The flips and flops of this case, which wend all the way to the Supreme Court, are enough to make your head spin. The fundamental issue that went to the Supreme Court in 2008 was whether the navy broke the law by not following relevant environmental legislation. The majority sidestepped, and instead stressed the importance of judicial deference to military judgments. "Forcing the navy to deploy an inadequately trained antisubmarine force jeopardizes the safety of the fleet," wrote Chief Justice John Roberts, reversing the lower court's ruling.

The bout of lawsuits did not resolve the question of navy due diligence and whether sufficient safeguards were being implemented to avoid harm to marine mammals—whether federal law was being violated, in essence—and so environmental groups kept the legal heat on. In a landmark 2015 settlement of two lawsuits between the navy and NRDC, the navy committed to adopt significant new safeguards in waters that encompassed the San Clemente Island Range Complex—safeguards that included restricting entirely or limiting significantly the use of mid-range sonar in areas designated as important to the survival of blue whales, beaked whales, and other threatened and endangered marine mammals.

As the navy aggressively pursued relief from environmental laws, it was also aggressively funding peer-reviewed research into sonar's effects on marine mammals. Beginning in 2000, the Office of Naval Research initiated the Marine Mammal Monitoring on Navy Ranges program to study responses to navy activities and to provide baseline population and habitat usage data in order to better help the navy do risk analysis. It hired world-class scientists as principal investigators who, in 2013, published results from a multiyear Southern California Behavioral Response Study that found that mid-frequency sonar deleteriously impacted blue whales and beaked whales—pretty much what environmental groups had been saying all along.

The US Navy funded 25 percent of all federal marine mammal research and mitigation in 2015 and a goodly amount of research conducted worldwide as well. Each year, according to the Defense Department, the navy spends between $10 million and $15 million to support universities and nonprofit organizations doing research into how sonar affects marine life in order to help combat its negative effects. The sonar research has led to important new discoveries beyond the effects on marine mammals' behavior. The studies have also revealed insights into the properties of sonar itself, how mammals use and are affected by sonar, and how nature can be tapped to inform next-generation technologies.

Even some of the navy's worthiest opponents on the sonar issue applaud the scientific rigor of the navy-funded research. Zak Smith is a senior attorney at NRDC specializing in marine mammals and has been involved in many of his organization's fiercest court battles with the navy. "We have found the science to be fairly sound, and the results of the studies to be very interesting and compelling. I mean, the science is always cautious, but that's the nature of science itself," he tells me when we meet at NRDC's fancy LEED-platinum building in Santa Monica. "To the navy's credit, although there has been an expansion of activity—the training tempo has gone up—the science has also gotten better, to where we know there are more impacts than we used to think. Also, the navy is getting more comprehensive in the universe of activities it covers in its environmental impact statements, which is a good thing."

Smith believes in the importance of the stick to compel stewardship on the part of the navy. "The National Environmental Policy Act, the Marine Mammal Protection Act, the Endangered Species Act, all these laws developed out of an understanding that there was a need for them, and that understanding was not solely housed in Congress in the 1970s," he says. He also acknowledges a growing environmental ethic within the military ranks. "The navy is not some behemoth. It is made up of men and women—some have families—who live in communities and who value clean air, clean water, whale watching, things like that. I take them at their word that people who work for the navy want to be good stewards."

San Clemente Island's first natural resources manager, Jan Larsen, believes that regardless of why the navy has undertaken environmental stewardship, its ongoing efforts will not be easily derailed by a changing naval hierarchy or political climate. Says Larsen, "I really doubt that the navy would change course. That's not to say it couldn't happen, but we've had too many environmental successes—across the services, not just the navy—to pull back now and say, 'We can't do this.'"

During the run-up to and early months of the Iraq War, a raft of military men testified before congressional committees that federally mandated species and habitat protections on Defense Department lands compromised combat readiness. In 2004 the military was granted a new National Defense Exemption to the Endangered Species Act, which should give one pause about just how embedded in the culture our landmark environmental legislation is.

Yet it's also important to note that the secretary of defense has had the power since the early years of the act to gain broad exemptions for "reasons of national security" but has, to date, never exercised that power—and so questions as to what "reasons of national security" actually means have never been tested in court. Even over the course of George W. Bush's presidency, the concept of national security shifted. In his 2002 National Security Strategy document, environmental destruction is not mentioned as a threat; in 2006 it absolutely is. Bush's 2006 National Security Strategy states that environmental destruction is "not [a] traditional national security concern, such as the conflict of arms or ideologies. But if left unaddressed [it] can threaten national security." Even during the fog of war, powerful advocates in the Bush administration saw the lifeline connecting natural and national security. Importantly, they understood how its rupture could impact the geopolitical balance.

Striking a cautious note of optimism, a former Pentagon official who worked closely with President Barack Obama's navy secretary Ray Mabus on energy and environmental issues told me that regardless of who's in the White House, "I really do believe that on the uniform side there's a huge amount of buy-in" on these issues. Our environmental legislation will always be vulnerable to anti-future ideologies such as those that question the need for regulation or the fact of human-influenced climate change, and so it is no small solace that the nexus between national and natural security is understood on the uniform side. Some in the armed services may chafe at Nixon's environmental legacy, including his establishment of the Environmental Protection Agency in 1970, as well as his signing of Pete McCloskey's three landmark pieces of environmental legislation, but as one marine put it, "We are by the book." The military is good at following orders, which in this case means that as long as environmental protection is the law of the land, the military will continue to keep faith with the future.

CHAPTER 5

THE DESERT TORTOISE
GETS AN ADDRESS CHANGE

MARINE CORPS AIR GROUND COMBAT CENTER
TWENTYNINE PALMS

Twentynine Palms is a quirky Mojave Desert town of about twenty-five thousand inhabitants located a few hours east of Hollywood. The latest movie releases are shown at the Smith's Ranch drive-in theater, an unpaved cash-only establishment surrounded by palm trees and the wide-open sky. Murals depicting larger-than-life Indian maidens, town founders, warfighters, and charismatic wildlife cover the sides of buildings along the business strip near Smith's Ranch while just out of town an old rabbit farm has been reconstituted as an art gallery named the Glass Outhouse. The eponymous facility next to the gallery is built with reflective material and contains a fully functioning flush toilet. When I use it I'm able to peer in 360 degrees at the arid landscape and at my husband and friends; I wave to them, but they can't see in.

The 1,200-square-mile Joshua Tree National Park borders Twentynine Palms on the town's south side. Serious hikers, day-trippers, and car-bound passers-through all enjoy the park's vast, stark, and year-round beauty. More than 2.5 million people visited the park in 2016. When I last hiked there about ten years ago, I passed two twentysomething guys with wind-whipped hair in the happy throes of psilocybin. I know because they told me. They also told me the name of their friend, tripping as well and straggling a few minutes behind them. "His name's Mike," one said. "Call him by name and start talking to him like you know him when you cross paths on the trail!" He was laughing so hard he could barely get out the request. I obliged when I saw Mike, which, as planned, totally freaked him out.

North of town is more crew cut. On the main drag, barbershops advertise razor fades and other military styles that adhere to the Marine Corps' "bulk of hair" limitations (parts are authorized but have to be off-center). Past the murals, Smith's Ranch, motorcycle shops, and vacant storefronts indicating that the economy is not thriving here, the road dead-ends at the Marine Corps Air Ground Combat Center. Clocking in at 1,100 square miles, the combat center is just a touch smaller than Joshua Tree, and the world's largest Marine Corps training installation. Commands based here include the Seventh Marine Regiment, which deployed to Kuwait for Operation Iraqi Freedom and fought pitched battles in Fallujah and Ramadi in Al Anbar Province. One of the town murals celebrates the fact that forty thousand people came out for a parade welcoming troops home after Desert Storm in 1991.

Between nature lovers, down-and-out desert dwellers, off-roaders, and warfighters, this part of the Mojave is animated by competing interests that do not always see eye to eye. The combat center is ground zero for several of these clashes.

There have been occasions when the installation's decisions ally it with conservationists: For example, in an effort to enhance the range and genetic diversity of certain species, the combat center helped the Mojave Desert Land Trust purchase 623 acres near Twentynine Palms in 2013. Containing thousands of Joshua trees and a lot of good habitat, the parcel was spared having 2,400 homes built on it and instead is now a living link between Joshua Tree National Park and the base, creating a "wildlife corridor" that makes it easier for animals to more safely range between the two large low-population areas. The corridor is designed to erase boundaries. If successful, it will become a planned "desire path," a term for how routes and shortcuts—whether goat trail or human footpath—usually form spontaneously and foster further use because travelers learn (or intuit) the route's utility. The Marine Corps' $700,000 contribution—more than half the cost of the land—came from the Readiness and Environmental Protection Integration Program, a Pentagon initiative that helps protect acreage near military bases so that a buffer is created against further encroachment.

Other decisions aren't so popular with the outdoor crowd. The most recent eruption of tensions occurred when the base expanded with the passage of the National Defense Authorization Act of 2014. Several key sections of the law fulfilled the wish of the Marine Corps, which in 2006 announced that, post-9/11, new threats combined with the development of new high-powered weaponry required additional terrain on which to train and test. With the Johnson Valley expansion, the Marines gained thousands of acres of adjacent public lands controlled by the Bureau of Land Management on which to practice live-fire shooting and bombing as well as infantry and tank maneuvers. This addition forever changed the contours of the base and the way it prepares for far-flung conflicts; it may also have changed the survival prospects for *Gopherus agassizii*, the federally listed desert tortoise.

First utilized by the army to train glider crews in the 1940s, what is now the combat center remained fairly quiet until the Marine Corps took control of the lands in 1952. In addition to the annual live-fire, combined arms, and maneuvers training for forty-five thousand sailors, marines, and foreign forces, it hosts the Marine Corps Communication-Electronics School. The technical school, which began in 1932 as the Pigeon and Flag Handler Platoon, moved from Quantico in 2014 and trains five thousand enlisted men and women annually. The combat center also provides a place for the FBI and a number of other federal and state agencies to conduct explosive-ordnance-disposal training.

Although there's a lot going on, only about 1 percent of the combat center's land has buildings on it. The majority of the base likely looks much as it did when the Serrano and Chemehuevi people lived there until they were forcibly relocated in the nineteenth century. The combat center's relatively unspoiled terrain is an aberration in the Mojave Desert. The population in surrounding communities has grown wildly: Between 1970 and 2014, Twentynine Palms grew 357 percent; nearby Yucca Valley grew 452 percent during the same period. More than eighteen million people live in the adjacent Greater Los Angeles metropolitan area, with recreationists escaping that urban sprawl only adding to the desert's ecological stress. That's not to say encroachment hasn't impacted the installation: The degradation, fragmentation, and destruction of overall Mojave Desert habitat has serious implications for how the military can train on the land it controls. Increased human population has led to the crash of some species populations, most notably those of the desert tortoise, thereby transforming the base into a de facto sanctuary.

The desert tortoise is amazingly adaptive: By burrowing into the soil with its evolutionarily fortified forelimbs and claws it can weather extremes of cold and heat—from 0 to above 110 degrees. It spends a lot of time in that burrow, up to 95 percent of its life by some estimates. Researchers have found that the burrowed tortoise can survive long periods of inactivity in its subterranean home by seriously reducing its metabolism. It can even inhale moisture from the surrounding dirt and, more amazingly, go up to two years without a proper drink of water. Various studies have found that the female of the species can store sperm to fertilize her eggs for at least three and perhaps up to ten years. The carapace of the desert tortoise is both armor against predators and a calendar: Like the turtles prevalent in the American Great Plains region and in Canada, the thirteen large segments on the animals' shells represent the thirteen moons of the lunar year to many Native Americans.

The animal has survived in this region for more than five million years because of its adaptability, but it's in trouble now. In 1990, the US Fish and Wildlife Service determined that the Mojave population of the desert tortoise was "threatened" throughout its range (north and west of the Colorado River in Arizona, Utah, Nevada, and California), due mostly to urban sprawl, with its attendant road-building and off-road-vehicle recreation, but also to an infectious and deadly upper-respiratory-tract disease, and to predators like ravens and coyotes. In addition to the listing, the service wrote a binding biological opinion outlining steps to reduce desert tortoise mortality and promote recovery.

Since the Department of Defense controls some of the desert tortoise's last best habitat, it has taken the lead in following the biological opinion to help improve the species' prospects. From its program aimed at boosting the desert tortoise population, to its $65 million desert tortoise research and relocation program, which began in 2011 and will last thirty years, the Marine Corps today is profoundly intertwined with the fortunes of the California state reptile. The base's Natural Resources and Environmental Affairs Department and the biologists contracted by the Department of Defense are devoted to the effort and determined that the desert tortoise not go the way of that other charismatic state mascot, *Ursus artcos californicus*, the California grizzly bear, which by 1922 had been completely exterminated by the advancing hordes of civilization.

THE DESERT TORTOISE also gets an assist from the combat center's Conservation Law Enforcement Officers, or CLEOs, led by Russell Elswick. The former soldier and street cop wears a gun and a two-way radio in holsters on his belt. Physically fit, he holds himself upright, chest a little alpha-puffed, and presents as the type of guy you wouldn't want to mess with, so I'm hit with a bit of cognitive dissonance when he responds effusively to a question about his conservation work: "I like being in the field, and seeing everything from the desert tortoise and the whiptail lizards to the little squirrels whose populations explode in a wet year. There's nothing like the smell of the desert when a storm rolls through, how before the raindrops hit the wind blows in your face and you smell that sweet damp smell. Seeing the flowers bloom. I get to enjoy what I protect and protect what I enjoy," he says.

In the vast majority of cases, Elswick tells me, his headaches don't come from the marines and sailors he and his three CLEOs interact with. "We tell thousands of marines that come through here every year what a tortoise is and what it looks like and what to do if they see one." The way Elswick sees it, there are forty-five thousand people in the field who can help protect desert tortoises on the base. His problem is with trespassers.

During the hotter parts of the year there aren't a lot of incursions, Elswick says, "but during the cooler months we can have a hundred-plus unauthorized people coming in on motorcycles, ATVs, and the like. We try to redirect them before they get to where they're disturbing our desert tortoises or our marines during training. When they enter from the west side, especially, they are likely to enter our high-density desert tortoise areas. These individuals are surface disturbing. They run over the desert tortoise's burrows. They affect the habitat. We can't have that."

Elswick adds that many are just out for a joyride and get off track, but others aren't so innocent. In a category that he says rises and falls with the nation's economic fortunes, Elswick has to deal with people who scavenge for the valuable detritus of simulated combat. Each year, tens of thousands of military men and women engage in training exercises. Spent ammunition from high-caliber rifles and machine guns; casings from illumination mortars; missile fins; and detonated hand grenades litter the desert after a day of live-fire training. Even before the Johnson Valley expansion, 175,000 tons of ordnance was dropped annually in designated areas of the base. That's a lot of metal, and it's valuable.

Scrapping on a live-fire range is not the smartest move. Scrappers have no idea when an area is "hot," meaning weapons are being fired, or where the unexploded ordnance might be. But at nearly a dollar a pound, collecting scrap metals like brass and aluminum is apparently worth the risk. Scrappers are subject to the authority of the base's military provost marshal's office, but Elswick and his CLEOs—all of whom are civilians—frequently come in contact with them first by default when they are on patrol. "Typically the scrappers are from the surrounding high desert, from socially and economically depressed areas. They're a little bit more desperate and a lot of them have criminal backgrounds. They're not going to be driving a Mercedes-Benz or off-road vehicle down our roads. They're driving, like, a '73 Lincoln Continental with mismatched tires. We see the gamut," Elswick says.

The scrappers may get a trunkful of metal, but the vast majority is collected by official crews and delivered to the base's Qualified Recycling Program facility. The only one of its size and scope operated on a military installation, the facility was a response to a challenge: In 2000 President Bill Clinton signed an executive order to green the government through federal environmental leadership. The combat center innovated further after President Obama's 2009 executive order to federal agencies to lead by example and come up with cutting-edge sustainability strategies.

Today, the facility recycles more than 170 types of matériel. What's brought in by the marines is sorted in a yard that's bare-boned but efficient and well organized. Even when desert temperatures reach 120 degrees, operators dressed head to foot in flame-retardant suits operate the facility's hellish outside furnace. The brass is melted in the furnace, as is copper, aluminum, and zinc. Then the metals are poured into molds, cooled, and sold off base. The facility pulls in revenues of $1.2 million annually, enough to employ six operators and two supervisors full time; to make the overall program self-sustaining; and to contribute hundreds of thousands of dollars per year to services that help improve the quality of life for marines and their families on base. It also puts a serious dent in the base's waste stream and its potential to contaminate underground water sources.

"Everybody is familiar with household recycling: your plastic bottles, aluminum cans, cardboard and stuff, but they're not familiar with this," says facility supervisor Palani Paahana. A big man with a sheaf of tattoos on his left forearm, Paahana gets a kick out of giving me a pair of souvenir brass balls. He scoops them from a line of bins that when full weigh 80,000 pounds—a lot of melted bullets. "They get made into candlestick holders, doorknobs, things like that." Each year, it keeps more than 8,000 tons of matériel out of the landfill, he says.

The recycling facility is a little steampunk, with its wood chippers reconstituted as hammer mills to transform brass bullets into marketable little balls; and it's a testament to human ingenuity and the will to problem-solve. That same spirit animates those tasked with figuring out how to save the Mojave's desert tortoise, though for this group it's still a work in progress.

KEN NAGY, A BIOLOGY PROFESSOR EMERITUS at UCLA's College of Life Sciences, has been studying the desert tortoise on various military bases since 2005. He was part of a team that helped implement the military's first desert tortoise Head Start–like programs—at the army's Fort Irwin National Training Center and at Edwards Air Force Base, both in the Mojave near Twentynine Palms and located in prime desert tortoise habitat. The plan was for biologists to collect pregnant females from the desert and provide an environment where they could lay their eggs unmolested. Females usually dig a hole, lay their eggs, and leave right away, so after the eggs hatched the females would be returned to the wild and the babies would be raised in enclo-sures until their shells were of a firmness and size—usually 4.5 inches, which takes about nine years in captivity—that made them less vulnerable to predators like ravens. The goal was to bolster declining populations of desert tortoises by giving the young ones a leg up, or head start. In the last forty years, des-ert tortoise populations in the western Mojave have declined by as much as 90 percent. The challenge was that the population decline had happened precipitously, so Nagy and the team had to scramble. They'd be developing new research protocols for head-starting and making new science as they went.

Nagy grew up poor in Venice Beach in the 1940s, staying mostly to himself and catching lizards and snakes in the salt marsh that is now Marina del Rey. A navy veteran, today he keeps the kid in him alive as a merit badge counselor for the Boy Scouts, overseeing environmental science, mammalogy, and bugling badges. He also keeps hold of that youthful won-der about how nature works. In his early years as a physiolog-ical ecologist, he studied, among other things, lizard pee—an odd-seeming choice until Nagy explains that grokking the tech-nical details of how lizards and the desert tortoise alter their metabolisms to survive in harsh circumstances may one day improve our understanding of how to survive on a trip to Mars.

Nagy continues to be a serious scientist but with a morbid sense of humor, referring to baby desert tortoises as "walking ravioli" because they make bite-size and tasty treats for pred-ators. Early missteps in his project included placing protec-tive netting over only part of the facility. This left an opening that ravens and hawks swooped through to grab babies at will. "Oops. Lesson learned," Nagy says. Overwatering created the next bit of mayhem, in that it encouraged an explosion of fire ants that killed and ate juveniles and eggs. "Turns out fire ants only become aggressive and carnivorous when their populations explode. When the soil is wet for a long time, they start breeding like crazy and little colonies break out all over the place, like measles on the surface of the ground."

"We got through that, and then the ground squirrels just kind of showed up one day," Nagy continues grimly. The new netting kept the ravens and hawks at bay, and flashing that started about a foot up the cyclone fence kept the coyotes, kit foxes, and other digging predators from getting in. But some kind of light must have blinked on in the ground squirrels' nut-size brains, because suddenly they began squeezing through the diamond-shaped fencing. "We thought they were omnivorous, but they hadn't been on the list of predators. Now they are."

It's hard trying to save a species from extinction. Lydia Millet, a novelist and conservationist, had it right when she observed in her essay "Good Grief" how few of the characteristics of gods we humans actually possess. "We're the living and the changing and the fallible. Our only true magic may lie in the gift of self-awareness: an awareness of our limits as well as our powers."

The US military is a war-fighting machine not known for humility, walking lightly, or philosophical reflection. Yet, due to the anthropogenic wages of progress, and by dint of geography and farsighted environmental law, it has been forced to adjust when it comes to the desert tortoise—the protection of which requires an awareness of relationships, cause and effect, and unintended consequences. Careful observation, data-gathering, and consultation before action must also come into play, as must long-term planning, multidisciplinary input, and an intimate knowledge of place.

Nagy's decades-long collaboration with the military

continues at the combat center, which runs the only remaining head-starting facility for the desert tortoise on Defense Department lands. The military loves its acronyms, and the Twentynine Palms operation, established in 2005, is referred to as TRACRS (pronounced "tracers"), for Tortoise Research and Captive Rearing Site.

ONE ADVANTAGE OF picking a "loser" in the existential sense is that it's easier to get a job in your field—particularly if that loser is charismatic. The man who runs TRACRS and the overall desert tortoise project on base is Brian Henen, a civilian with a Ph.D. in physiological ecology and one of Nagy's former Ph.D. students. Two days after Henen finished his Ph.D. fieldwork in 1989, the desert tortoise was temporarily listed as endangered. Within the year it was formally listed as threatened. Henen has been busy ever since.

Although habitat loss, degradation, and fragmentation have had the heaviest impact on the desert tortoise, there has been a pile-on effect caused by prolonged drought; the spread of disease; and predation. In addition to these odds against thriving, there is the complication inherent to desert tortoise biology: The animal requires fifteen to twenty years to reach sexual maturity but experiences relatively high mortality early in life due to the aforementioned threats. In short, recovery is not a given.

"It gets complicated really fast and it's difficult to figure out how to manage," Henen acknowledges. Head-starting desert tortoises has been seen as one potential way to replenish the population. But it's no panacea; it's not even a sure bet. "Our aim is to determine if head-starting can work," offers Henen, who's been at the combat center since 2006 but linked to the recovery effort since he assisted Nagy at the previous head-starting programs on other bases. Annual survivorship of babies and juveniles inside Henen's facility is approximately 85 to 96 percent, he says, compared to about 40 percent or less in the wild. The Mojave National Preserve thought enough of Henen's head-starting efforts to base its own desert tortoise recovery program on his design and protocols at TRACRS. But it's still too early to tell whether any of this will work: Desert tortoises can live to the age of eighty in the wild, so it won't be known for many years how well the human-raised animals fare long term after release.

On September 30, 2015, Henen and his team released the first set of juveniles born and raised in his enclosure. Of the 475 juveniles reared in the facility, 35 were gauged to be of sufficient size to be safely released. They were nine years old. The facility made its second tortoise release in the spring of 2017 when 50 juveniles were released into a non-live-fire training area.

Biologists on Henen's team closely monitor head-start releases via radio transmitters and GPS tracking, which is how they know that in the two years since the first release, 18 out of 35 have survived so far. Most of the mortalities are due to coyotes, which attack tortoises of any size. According to Henen, the yearly survival rate is about 65 percent, which approximately matches what researchers think is the survival rate in the wild—although there's not a lot of data on that. None of the released juveniles have been killed by ravens, though. Henen thinks this is a good indication that they're releasing them at the right size.

Henen has the affect and demeanor of Mr. Rogers: He's folksy and gentle, with an intelligence that is not showy but grounded in observation and experience. He's also a scientist who does not hide his affection for his four-legged charges. Henen has a pet desert tortoise of his own named Rabbit, who was adopted from a rescue center in Nevada. It's estimated that there are eighty-five thousand Mojave Desert tortoises remaining in the wild, but in a sign of just how imperiled the species is, Las Vegas is believed to have the greatest concentration—most of them pets or in rescue centers. That kind of downer fact might lead one to wonder whether it's worth even trying to save the species. Here, too, climate change is altering habitat, as it is with the endangered San Clemente Island loggerhead shrike. But consider this: Although the desert tortoise spends the bulk of its life in the burrow it painstakingly digs in the hardened desert soil, its burrow does not shelter it alone. More than 150 other species "squat" in those burrows as well, and depend on them for survival. Burrowing owls, for instance, are frequent freeloaders in desert tortoise burrows. As an integral part of the Mojave Desert ecosystem, the tortoise's decline shakes the biotic chain of life.

IT REMAINS A MATTER of unsettled science whether the desert tortoise recognizes the particular neighborhood in which it burrows, or its neighbors for that matter. The jury is still out on whether it has a strong homing instinct, so that when moved it tries to return to its burrow rather than habituate itself to its new surroundings and neighbors. The head-starting program hasn't answered this research question. Pregnant females are geospatially tagged when taken from their habitat in the wild and then returned to the exact spot once they've hatched their eggs at TRACRS. The recently released juveniles have so far fared as well as those hatched in the wild. It's another more controversial base effort that will inevitably address this and other important research questions regarding the desert tortoise.

With the passage of the 2014 National Defense Authorization Act, the combat center expanded into a large swath of Bureau of Land Management territory in Johnson Valley adjacent to the base. Much of the land is great desert tortoise habitat and also a long-favorite destination for off-roaders. At around 200,000 acres, Johnson Valley was the largest off-highway-vehicle area in the United States. Under the new law—the particulars of which were fiercely contested—about 43,000 acres will remain open to off-roaders, and an additional 53,000 acres will be "borrowed" by the Marine Corps twice a year, for a total of sixty days, for training exercises. The remaining 107,000 acres will be controlled by the Department of the Navy, made off-limits to the public, and used to train large-scale Marine expeditionary brigades for heavy-duty air and ground action.

In anticipation of the expansion, Henen and Alice Karl, a contracted biologist with thirty years of experience researching the desert tortoise, headed studies of contingencies and then developed plans for how and where to move the animals out of harm's way before training in the newly acquired areas began. Each year for the past three and a half years, crews conducted detailed field surveys: Up to 110 biologists walked back and forth, 10 meters apart, twice covering each square kilometer of the withdrawal area in order to find as many desert tortoises as possible. More than a thousand were found. If an animal was bigger than about 4.5 inches—the size of the head-started graduates—the surveyors assigned it a number and marked that number on its shell, used epoxy glue to attach a radio transmitter, and then left the animal in place. Anything smaller wouldn't hold a transmitter, so about 250 juveniles were moved to a separate enclosure at the TRACRS facility.

Off-highway-vehicle enthusiasts and environmental groups

were not happy. Of the "scoping" comments received from the public during the deliberative process, 71 percent came from off-roaders and 21 percent from conservationists. The OHV crowd was exercised that a big chunk of their playground was taken from them, but it was the navy's proposal to "translocate" desert tortoises from the newly acquired land to other, less-trafficked habitat on the base and adjacent BLM territory that elicited the strong conservation reaction. The initial Desert Tortoise Translocation Program proposal also raised serious concerns among biologists in the US Fish and Wildlife Service, which is responsible for approving environmental permits. In 2016 the plan—still being revised based on public and Fish and Wildlife comments—also triggered a "Notice of Intent to Sue" by the Center for Biological Diversity, an aggressive and litigiously successful conservation advocacy organization. The center warned it would follow through unless significant changes were made. Henen and Karl put the March 2016 translocation goal on hold and got to work on the supplemental environmental impact statement, reinstating the consultative process with Fish and Wildlife and attempting to address the center's concerns. In the end, by all accounts, Henen and his colleagues came up with a better—though not perfect—plan.

Ileene Anderson, senior scientist and Public Lands Deserts Director at the center, has been critical of the translocation plan from the get-go. "There are actually not that many listed species in the desert, but one that is wide ranging and relatively charismatic and continuing its march toward extinction is, unfortunately, the desert tortoise," she says. Among the concerns she and the center voiced were the animal's still-not-fully-understood homing instinct and its ability to habituate to a new burrow before being picked off by predators. They also didn't like the five-year monitoring commitment. "So they monitor for five years and after that it's, 'Whatever happened to those guys? Did they ever reproduce?'"

When I first spoke to her she described the expansion as a martial bait and switch. "I believe the military guys don't want to have to deal with them, don't want to have to constantly be talking to Fish and Wildlife about how many they have killed when they're doing their war games. It would be onerous. Tanks are not your typical off-road vehicle, and so there would undoubtedly be much more mortality [if the tortoises stayed in Johnson Valley]. So they want to move them."

Although still troubled about how translocation might deleteriously impact the animals, Anderson says, the center decided in the end not to sue because the 2017 revised translocation plan addressed many of its concerns. The center's lawyers decided it would be "very unlikely that they would be able to prevail" in court, she explains.

The new plan stretches monitoring from five years—what the Fish and Wildlife Service generally requires in its permitting process—to thirty years. "We've never had a project proponent commit to thirty years of monitoring. In fact, I don't know of any other species that has ever had that kind of long-term monitoring," Anderson says. In short, the navy went above and beyond the usual permitting requirements—based on conservation concerns voiced by groups like Anderson's. The initial plan had also failed to identify where on BLM territory the desert tortoises would be moved to, how many would be moved, how many already lived there, and whether there was healthy habitat enough for all. "The language was very, very vague," and the center strongly protested, Anderson says. The new plan is downright granular.

Anderson notes that the combat center also committed to increasing its Conservation Law Enforcement Officer presence in the translocation areas—adding two CLEOs to Elswick's four-person force in 2016—especially during long weekends popular with off-road enthusiasts. The CLEOs will patrol both recipient and control sites at least ten times per year, and can supplement on-the-ground law enforcement with helicopter patrols. They will also look for off-road vehicle travel, and desert collections of trash, which attract ravens and coyotes—the desert tortoises' main predators.

The Center for Biological Diversity did not get all it wanted from the combat center. The translocation was green-lighted, for one thing. But on some of the important issues, Anderson acknowledges that the combat center and the Department of the Navy "stepped up to the plate."

ON A CLEAR SPRING DAY in April 2017, the great desert tortoise translocation commenced. Long before this day arrived, biologists had pinpointed where in Johnson Valley each of the 1,043 "transmittered" desert tortoises to be moved were located. They had studied the species' native habitat and plotted its destination to one of four translocation sites based on how closely the new area replicated the geologic features and soil type of its Johnson Valley home. Was its burrow in a valley, an alluvial fan, or a bajada? Gently sloping? Sandy? Loamy? Was there an outcropping or sizable tree in sight? They also studied the social structure around the desert tortoise. Whole "neighborhoods" would be moved together, and in the same geospatial relationship, to keep the social structure intact and, it was hoped, decrease the desert tortoise's homing tendency. The few extant studies on desert tortoises and homing had found that in the first two years after an animal is moved it is more active above ground, making it more susceptible to predation, but in year three it tends to settle into its new habitat. Decreasing those early urges to meander looking for familiar sights and smells is thereby seen as a critical translocation strategy.

Henen had been working on one version or another of the translocation plan since 2011, and now, finally, he was one of the leads orchestrating the work of 125 biologists, making sure that all of the animals were safely moved. Each tortoise would be radio-located in the wild and placed in a Sterilite bin with air holes drilled into the side. A form would be filled out on the spot with the biologist's name, tortoise's ID number, capture date, capture time, and geolocation of the capture, then replaced in the plastic sleeve on top of the bin. The bins—five max per trip— would be loaded onto a backpack and hiked by the biologist to a mobile health-assessment and processing station—which would move on to new sites as the host quadrants were emptied.

When I arrive in the expansion area of Johnson Valley to observe day five of the thirteen-day operation, 266 animals had already been airlifted to their new habitat. The health-assessment station is set up on the south side of Bessemer Mine Road—a veterinary version of a MASH unit, with syringes to draw blood or rehydrate the animal, bags of human-grade sodium chloride, weight scales, and very focused biologists wearing blue plastic gloves. One of them, an Austrian, is a Ph.D. and world-renowned turtle and tortoise expert by the name of Peter Praschag. He founded Turtle Island, a turtle conservation breeding and research center in Graz, Austria, and was the subject of a 2016 German documentary titled *Turtle Hero*. Praschag and his conservation-center partner Shannon DiRuzzo, a veterinarian, work smoothly together at the makeshift examination table—with his accent and air of quiet authority lending a touch of the surreal to the Mojave Desert scene. On the table is Tortoise MC2013, though DiRuzzo says I can call him Bob if I want to. Bob is big, too big for the scale on hand, so another has to be pulled from the truck to weigh him. "Six point three kilograms, an exceptionally large male," confirms Praschag, apparently impressed. On average, adult desert tortoises weigh 3.6 to 6.8 kilograms (8 to 15 pounds).

After the turtle is weighed DiRuzzo frees the transmitter from Bob's shell. Not all of the translocated animals will be tracked, but 20 percent will—more than were proposed in the first translocation plan. In the new plan, 225 translocated tortoises, 225 animals already resident in the areas to which the newcomers will be translocated, and 225 in a control population will be tracked. All told, those desert tortoises will be tracked in the first twenty-four hours of the translocation, then twice a week for the first two weeks, and then every week during their active season (March–October) and once or twice a month during the rest of the year. The base is only committed to this level of tracking for five years and will, at that time, reevaluate, "to see if that's overkill," according to Henen. But tracking will continue for thirty years. Among the potential research benefits of this effort, Henen and his team hope to learn more about homing: whether it's even a thing, how far the animals range if it is, and how they might mitigate the effect. Because this is long term, they'll find out whether the animals integrate well into the host population and whether the females mate with new neighbors or just utilize the sperm they are capable of carrying. The research potential is rich.

"This is a very badly behaved male. He's not very happy

about this exam," notes Praschag after Bob peed on the examination table—a big deal in the desiccated universe in which the desert tortoise dwells. The animal's adaptive physiology makes it possible for it to go exceedingly long stretches without a drink of water—but that only works if it doesn't urinate, which it tends to do if spooked. Every single animal that is translocated must be rehydrated. There's even a place on the individual tortoise's translocation form marked REHYDRATE that must be filled in with when, by what method, how much, and by whom.

After Bob and his neighbors are assessed and processed, they await the move to the airlift area. The forms on each bin are already jammed with information, but now there is also colored tape across them, with black marker notations of the neighborhood group to be airlifted, the name of the drop-off site (for example, SIB was Siberia, a remote location on BLM-managed land north of the base), the exact GPS coordinate of where it will be placed at that site, and the name of the biologist who will do the placing.

At the airlift site, a group of about fifty occupied bins are stacked under a flapping blue tarp. Five million years of evolution for an animal that has to dig in soil sometimes as hard as concrete has created some fiercely strong forelimbs that are being utilized to butt up against the bin tops. Rocks the size of softballs are there to keep the lids on.

The Bell 47 helicopter approaches from the north and then slowly descends to the makeshift landing spot, kicking up a miniature dust storm. The compact red two-seater has been modified with long metal bins along the length of its landing runners to hold the precious cargo. When the chopper touches down the biologists swing into action. Bins are loaded one by one, in exact opposite order of how they will be off-loaded and

geospatially placed. Siberia, a big valley far from any population centers or OHV traffic on BLM land, is today's destination.
When loaded, the Bell 47 lifts straight into the air, then veers
north, the *thwapping* sound of its blades quickly fading.

Now, we wait and see if it all works out.

Animals migrate for myriad natural reasons, yet the combat
center's mass movement of desert tortoises is anything but. The
translocation of more than a thousand animals was forced on
nature by the requirements for testing ever-more-high-potency
weapons, for training increasing numbers of infantry in large-
scale desert combat, and because rapacious and seemingly
unchecked development has bulldozed so much of the desert
tortoise's fragile home range. The combat center's environmental department and its civilian biologists followed the law and
undertook a grand, even godly, effort to do least harm under
the circumstances. While many of us won't live long enough to
learn the results of thirty years of monitoring this complicated
and controversial endeavor, it may be fruitful to spend some
time now contemplating how we came to need the 2017 Great
Desert Tortoise Translocation in the first place.

CHAPTER 6

A RIVER RUNS THROUGH IT

MARINE CORPS BASE CAMP PENDLETON

Borders are funny things: two-sided and multidimensional; real enough to spark wars between nations when violated; but also ephemeral, like lines drawn in the sand. A border is at once impenetrable and porous, discrete and blurry, and perhaps no other military installation in Southern California more acutely represents this dual nature than Marine Corps Base Camp Pendleton.

The base is a secure federal military installation, hemmed in by the megalopolises of Los Angeles and San Diego and therefore holding the line against the kind of development devourment that's eaten up so much of California's coast. Traveling between the two cities on Interstate 5, there's one place where nature abounds with avian-festooned estuaries, vast swaths of untrammeled coastal sage scrub, and hills rolling and rising inland to disappear into the fog. It's the only stretch of that god-awful drive that's bearable, and when passing through those 125,000 verdant acres it's easy to forget it's a military installation where men and women prepare for combat. Approximately forty-five thousand tightly organized and executed training events occur there each year.

Yet, Camp Pendleton is also part of a much larger natural matrix. In its *State Wildlife Action Plan*, California's Department of Fish and Wildlife conceives Camp Pendleton and its neighbors as one South Coast province, characterized by the Mediterranean-type climate and the very particular amphibians, flora, and fauna natural to this place—mountain lions among them. Camp Pendleton is at the western end of the province's Santa Ana–Palomar Mountains Linkage, which contains the last remaining natural habitat connecting the coastal lowland to an inland chain of largely protected mountain ranges. Wide-ranging animals like mountain lions depend on these kinds of wildlife corridors for their continued existence here. One of those big cats had recently traveled through the base, as evidenced at a creek crossing in a steep drainage where I saw its fist-size tracks in the mud. Importantly, what also defines the province are the threats and stressors to its native wildlife and habitat, including growth and development; water misman-agement and the degradation of aquatic ecosystems; invasive species; fires unnatural in season, intensity, and impact; and recreationists loving accessible open spaces to death. Although mentioned in 2005, climate change was added to the list in a robust fashion in 2015.

The ecological interconnectedness of the region is best exem-plified by the Santa Margarita River, a life-sustaining system that flows unimpeded through two counties and is among the western United States' richest biodiversity hot spots. Through rugged canyons, an intensively urbanizing landscape, and the sparsely populated military base that is 80 percent undeveloped, the Santa Margarita flows freely southwest for 27 miles—the last

10 through Camp Pendleton. At the river's wide and beautiful mouth, the Santa Margarita empties into the Pacific. Its riparian corridor contains multitudes, including more than eleven hundred species of flora and fauna on the base alone: Many of the eighteen species federally listed as threatened and endangered on Camp Pendleton depend on the river for survival.

The installation's environmental stewards operate within this dynamic matrix where upstream actions can have downstream consequences and even third- and fourth-order effects. Understanding what threatens the landscape's integrity and dynamism; how to defeat, mitigate, or avoid those threats altogether; how apparently discrete parts are in fact connected; and how to heal scars and restore nature to health are fundamental to the base's highly coordinated stewardship effort. That type of matrix thinking is fundamental to Camp Pendleton's national security mission as well.

"A country worth defending is a country worth preserving," Major General Michael Lehnert had said to me at Camp Pendleton a decade ago as we stood at an overlook, taking in the unimpeded view of one of the base's river basins. As he said those words I was surrounded by marines in uniform, many from the base's Environmental Security Department. They'd probably heard Lehnert recite the phrase a lot, but it was new to me and it resonated. The nation was in the middle of the Iraq War at the time, and the political winds in Washington were chilly if not openly hostile toward the goal of conservation and environmental protection. Lehnert's commanding presence and commitment to both national and natural defense gave me a glimmer of hope, and a sense that the environmental movement had been overlooking a potentially powerful ally. If nothing else, the US military is apolitical and operationally decisive; it knows how to get things done. I'd traveled to installations all over Southern California and then back ten years later to Camp Pendleton, where it was confirmed: Both stewardship and the work of military preparedness can thrive. The unexpected surprise was that many of the organizing and animating principles by which they operate and succeed have a good deal in common.

WHEN THE LANDS for the base were acquired during World War II, thousands of acres of fertile floodplain were being used to grow row crops, among them vine-ripened tomatoes. Today, a 32,000-square-foot former tomato-packing plant is headquarters for a high-tech simulator that teaches both combat tactics and cultural awareness. The Infantry Immersion Trainer, which was opened a year after my initial visit in 2006, was the result of a request by a former commander of the Marine expeditionary force at Camp Pendleton, General James Mattis, now President Trump's secretary of defense. With no disrespect to Fort Irwin's impressive combat town, Camp Pendleton's immersion trainer is Ujen on high-tech steroids. It's run by a former Marine Corps combat veteran who lost men and women under his command, suffers from PTSD, writes poetry, and would likely have been as adept at the work of the earlier tomato farm as he is in this world of simulated urban warfare.

Robert Thielen learned to drive at age seven on his family's dairy operation in Eden Valley, Minnesota, "as soon as my legs were long enough to reach the clutch and the brakes on the tractor." He signed up with the Marines at eighteen, in 1979. "I wanted to see what was beyond the horizon of cornstalks in Eden Valley. I knew there had to be more out there." He was a machine gunner and a drill instructor. He did five tours of combat: one in Somalia and four in Iraq. He retired in 2009 a regiment sergeant major for the Fifth Marines. "I was struggling at the end. For about the last year and a half of the Marine Corps I was only sleeping two to four hours a night," he says.

When I first meet him I notice that his teal blue shirt matches his teal blue eyes, which are ringed with red. Fairly quickly I understand he is a man with a big but burdened heart. In 2010, when he first started working at the facility he now directs, the explosions, shooting, and smells triggered traumatic memories. "'Why am I so angry when I leave here?' I'd ask myself....I'd be driving home and a semitruck with a container on it would go over a bump and there'd be that loud boom. My chest got so tight. I'd be gasping for breath....I didn't watch any violent movies. Anything violent would bring stuff back. I'd watch chick flicks as an outlet for emotion and be crying on the couch," Thielen says.

When the Iraq war started in 2003, Thielen says the biggest threats to him and his unit were ill-trained marines accidentally blowing things up. By 2004, the insurgents had regrouped. "They came to Fallujah and we were getting bombed every day. They started using IEDs that blew up with a pressure plate, meaning that if I step on something or compress something it's going to make a connection with the wiring." Logistics figured that out and made the first mine roller to push in front of convoys to set off the buried IEDs. "But then the insurgents started using radio-controlled IEDs. They could use a washing machine timer, anything, to set it off. Technology changes tactics, tactics change technology. The battlefield is fluid. It's like a chess game."

Thielen's immersion trainer team interviews unit commanders about their objectives. Based on the scenario, he knows what they'll need: a pyrotechnician, explosives, rifles, interpreters in a specific language, actors, et cetera. The scenario planner then maps the scenes on a storyboard, keeping front and center the objectives the Marines want to train to. "We use a map of our facility, with symbols like 'population.' We will put our actors in those locations. We have 'atmospherics,' what we want to set visually for the marines to see. 'Disposition' is basically what our enemy will be doing." Thielen shows me a storyboard with a population, an IED set to explode, and two shooters symbolized by red dots with arrows pointing the direction they will move in the exercise. The storyboard can also denote where sound originates and moves, so that the *thwap* of helicopter blades will seem to be passing overhead.

The immersion process also includes scent machines able to pump out everything from trash rotting to tea brewing to corpses decomposing. The immersion trainer purchases these and other scents from the subsidiary of an American manufacturer far better known for household air fresheners, according to Thielen.

The $40 million facility conducts frequent "atmospheric refreshes" to keep up with changes in conflict location and tactics. Murder holes were not a problem for security patrols in Iraq, for example, but were everywhere in Afghanistan and are now a common feature in the immersion trainer. Animatronic figures programmed to interact with marines come with multiple detachable silicone faces and hands so that they can be fitted with skin tones that match the dominant ethnicity of a conflict zone. Programmers in a remote-control room watch the scenes via any number of the three hundred mounted cameras in the immersion trainer and can activate and also change the facial expressions on their animatronic figures to look angry, confused, scared. In one scenario, for example, a bike-shop figure can be made to pull a knife or pistol out of his clothing. He can throw a grenade or detonate an IED depending on his programming. He looks unsettlingly real and contains a chip that enables him to speak three different languages. His hair is hand sewn into his scalp, and his face, which has a brown skin tone, is held on by magnets.

The day I'm there, actors in one section of the large facility, which can accommodate several different combat units working with different scenarios, are speaking Tagalog. I had expected to hear the Pashto or Dari of Afghanistan, or the Arabic of Iraq, since those were the well-known hot spots in the news at the time. Instead, we are in the Philippines. Thielen shrugs when asked about the location. "That was what the unit wanted. So, they may be going somewhere in the Pacific," he says.

The military's intervention calculus is shrouded in mystery. I take note that four days after the Camp Pendleton visit, a *New York Times* headline reads, "Nearly 1,800 Killed in Duterte's Drug War, Philippine Police Official Tells Senators." I have not paid attention to President Rodrigo Duterte since his election three months earlier or, apparently, to ongoing efforts in the Philippines by US Army Special Forces to help combat militants allied to Islamic State. The Marine Corps has.

In another section, an avatar system is honing small-unit infantry skills. A holographic imam and two other figures are projected in front of a wall in a room deliberately designed to make participants feel uncomfortable. "It's meant to give an insecure feeling. We got that from our research and development folks. It's too small; it's too tight. We want people to feel trapped." It takes ten or fifteen seconds for a marine to open a door, move through a room, and assess whether there is a threat.

"We're trying to build muscle memory so they can focus on what's important," Thielen says. Cameras capture the scenario, and an after-action review allows participants to see how they've done. The video captures a marine being spooked by a movement in the shadows and shooting. A holographic figure drops to the earthen floor. It's an unarmed woman.

Outside the facility, yet another unit is conducting a security patrol in a simulated Afghan village full of street vendors. Actors hawking their wares in a foreign tongue look warily at the marines as the young men move through without speaking, on high alert. An interpreter accompanies them but is not asked to engage any of the townspeople. One marine spends the entire time moving ahead backward, as though he's sure his unit will be ambushed from behind.

During the after-action review, the unit commander and a facility trainer, standing in the center of a horseshoe-shaped conference table, review the behavior of the fourteen marines who sit around the table, their guns resting in front of them along with their upturned helmets. Name patches sewn onto the backs of their flak jackets read WHOLLEY, HALL, STYLES, PERROW. They look so young.

"Where were the murder holes?" the trainer asks. Silence. "You walked by five of them!"

A marine stares at the map projected on a screen at the front of the room. It shows their patrol area, with various numbers marking buildings and positions. "At sixteen, facing north," he finally says.

"Good! Next one?"

"Next one was in the six. There were two facing south."

"Outstanding."

The trainer punches up a video showing the Marine unit

walking down a narrow street in the combat village, a facsimile of a million dusty places in the developing world. Buildings crowd in on both sides. "There are a couple things we gotta start being aware of. Not one marine is covering the rooftops. I can't have everybody concentrating on the ground. That elevated position can cause a lot of trouble for foot patrols."

Thielen helped write the "concept of operations" for the Infantry Immersion Trainer. Although two other immersion trainers have been built—one at Marine Corps Base Hawaii and one at Camp Lejeune in North Carolina—Camp Pendleton's was the first and is still the most forward-leaning and experimental. Thielen's Iraq experiences were his guide: "If marines come into a village in a protective posture, or a hostile posture where their weapons are up, it would be like a policeman coming to your door pointing his gun at you. It's a big deal. So we practice that," he says. Potential pitfalls can be less obvious; an innocent act can have serious negative effects. Says Thielen, "Even something as simple as passing out soccer balls. Put yourself in a father's place. I gave his son a soccer ball and that was something he couldn't give him. Does he feel pride or shame in that? I need to think about possible consequences. I've insulted him. I could have given him the ball to give to his son so he doesn't lose face."

The squad leader rises. "Let's talk about your presence in that town. You were standoffish. Don't you think that's insulting, especially as it's your first time in the village? They're just trying to go about the business of their lives and you come in there and pretty much flip them off. You're creating enemies. If someone's trying to sell you something, say 'no thank you.' Say 'hi.' Learn at least that much of their language. If you try to learn their customs, courtesies, and language, that's going to go a very long way. You need to make connections. Trust me on that."

SHERRI SULLIVAN, WHO BEGAN working on base as a riparian biologist in 2007 and is now its head wildlife biologist, is all about connections. The wildlife staff under her direction is segregated by topography: upland, riparian, estuary/shore, and aquatic, but everyone is expected to know how their particular work fits into the whole. Camp Pendleton takes an ecosystem management approach that attempts to deal with the fabric of life rather than focus on discrete threads, which is one reason why Sullivan, a civilian with long blond hair and the mellow affect of a native San Diegan, works so closely with Deborah Bieber, head of the Land Management Section of Camp Pendleton's Environmental Security Department. They collaborate well and are too respectful to finish each other's sentences, but I get the feeling they probably could.

Sullivan has a deep knowledge of Camp Pendleton's fauna and its relationship to the habitat. We meet one late-February morning at Blue Beach, near the mouth of the Santa Margarita. The sun warms, though the breeze is cool and moist. The beach in front of us is deserted save for six brown pelicans that skim the surface of a cresting wave, heading south.

To the north, contractors are erecting temporary fencing and posting restriction signs in advance of bird breeding season. When Sullivan first arrived on base, the beach area had been pretty much flattened so that it could no longer do what nature intended, which is to have wind action form little undulating "foredunes" between the ocean and estuary to shelter nesting birds. There *were* no such foredunes, Sullivan says. So she and Bieber put their heads together and got to work.

The rules of their engagement originate in a 1995 Fish and

Wildlife biological opinion, which first set specific conservation and protection rules and mandated that the base come up with a plan, and then maintain or recover listed species on base. To make it work, the different sections of Camp Pendleton's Environmental Security team would have to work together. Bieber, who has been in the Land Management Section since 2001, oversees the updating and revision of the plan every five years in close collaboration with other section heads, including Sullivan.

When we meet at the beach so she can give me the lay of the land, the first thing Bieber does is plop herself down and take off her shoes. As we talk, she moves her bare feet around on the warming sand. She is at home out of doors but also kind of nerdy: She wears her dark glasses and her reading glasses at different levels on her forehead and goes back and forth between them when she wants to show me some particularly cool plant. "That 1995 document said that in order to offset impacts of military training to listed species like the California least terns and western snowy plovers, the base had to restore the dune system. That meant removing all the ice plant. Back then we had 100 percent cover of ice plant. That was before my time, but ice plant eradication was the prescription for restoring the dune system. What Pendleton contractors did, innocently, was spray the ice plant but leave it in place."

When Bieber came aboard the lands program in 2001, she read the plan and continued to treat the ice plant. But then she noticed that the treated areas left a lot of dead ice plant whose organic matter created upland-type soil instead of sand dune. "We were getting weeds because the organic matter was providing nutrients," Bieber recalls of the unintended consequences. The annual weeds would grow and die, grow and die, making more upland soil. Then the upland plants started coming in, growing, and dropping their leaves to create more organic matter.

"In our effort to create healthy dunes for our endangered species, we started losing big chunks of dunes system," she says. Weeding wasn't enough. They had to get rid of the entire top layer of organic matter. Slowly, slowly, a healthy dunes system began to form. Bieber's team has so far worked its way about 6 miles up the coast from Blue Beach, and converted over 200 weedy acres to resilient and sheltering dunes that two of the base's imperiled bird species use for breeding: the California least tern, which stands out in the scenery with its black crown, white body and face, and a beak that is long, pointy, and bright yellow, and the western snowy plover, a comparatively stocky little thing and sand colored.

Dunes are found at the confluence of rivers to the ocean, and Santa Margarita's are the largest and most healthy in the region, Sullivan explains, adding that after years of effort, "We now have both management for the terns and plovers [and] also management for the ecosystem. It's very rare anywhere else in San Diego County to see beautiful foredunes like we have here. It's as natural as we can make it look, and it's night and day to what it was."

Bird breeding season starts March 1, and the base is required by the biological opinion to have the dune fencing up by March 15 each year. The area would soon be populated by the nesting California least tern colony. The birds usually fly in around May, with peak breeding around June. When the California least tern was placed on the endangered species list in 1970, Camp Pendleton had just 19 nesting pairs at the mouth of the Santa Margarita, with only 225 nesting pairs total recorded in all of California.

Today, more than a thousand pairs nest seasonally in the Camp Pendleton colony.

Whereas the California least tern is pelagic, meaning it's an oceangoing bird that only comes to land to breed, the western snowy plover is a year-round resident. It flits and forages along the shore's seaweed-strewn wrack line and tends to like building its nest closer to its forage, which makes the nest and its contents more vulnerable both to tide washouts and to inadvertent trampling, since many of their nests are outside the protective fencing. The western snowy plover's sand-colored feathers don't help, either. Its coloration is an evolutionary trait great for camouflage but not great when you like to build your nest in sandy divots sometimes created by amphibious tank tracks.

Blue Beach is part of a concentrated 5-mile stretch containing threatened and endangered species; it's also an active amphibious training area part of the year. During breeding season, the Marine Corps shifts most training away from the beach, but during the winter it's bustling with water ops, amphibious-vehicle landings, and maneuvers. From late March to September, there is limited activity, mostly as a transition point along a set lane that connects ship-to-shore assault amphibious vehicles to interior training areas. Marines are trained to keep an eye out for plovers and terns, and the speed limit is 25 miles per hour on the beach, but on occasion a few birds are killed.

The two bird species are among the twelve threatened or endangered species that come under Sullivan's purview. "Each one is unique in its own way, but the beach provides a good focal point," she says. For starters, unlike most every other beach in Southern California, Camp Pendleton's are not groomed. "We don't pick up our seaweed to make it nice for people who want to recreate. That leaves a food source on the beaches, which is one of the reasons we have a comparatively large population of western snowy plovers."

The entire beach and dune area is mapped on a grid, and then the counting begins: "Every single nest is counted, then tracked to see if it was successful. We are finding banded adult birds on other installations that were born here. Sorry, bad biology! That *hatched* here and moved on," Sullivan says.

We drive to a spot coveted by birders—though mostly prohibited to them—on a high bank above the now wide Santa Margarita. Wisps of clouds pass above as a sweet-smelling breeze wafts in from the sea, mixing with the scents of coastal sage scrub and chaparral. It's a peaceful, exquisite, intoxicating scene that affords a clear view of the estuary—as close as we can get without disturbing the wildlife. Without binoculars we can only make out white dots on the sandbar, but they are myriad.

Sullivan and Bieber, as well as the biologists they supervise, are part of the human matrix that helps the Santa Margarita corridor stay vibrant. That matrix also includes universities, the San Diego Zoo, and the US Geological Survey, among others, which sign cooperative agreements with the base to do research there. For example, one scientist secured a grant from the State of California to tag California least terns at Camp Pendleton and track exactly where they winter as well as the migration routes they use to get there, and also what they eat. "They've put cameras out near the nests to see what kind of foods the terns are bringing," Sullivan says. "They've a hypothesis that because of global warming their food base is moving farther away, which means it takes them longer to pick up food to provision the chicks with." On the day I visit, the study's researchers are on the beach capturing and banding adult terns as part of the range-wide survey.

"We're promoting all kinds of science on Camp Pendleton

that is being used [to protect species] up and down the state,"
says Sullivan. Noting that if there are recovering species elsewhere pressure is lifted off the base, she adds, "It's to our benefit.
Plus, we take seriously our mandate to manage the land for the
public benefit."

Bieber says, "We're always trying to think of the big picture."

THE LOWER SANTA MARGARITA above the estuary is a wide strip of
fecundity amidst drought-tolerant coastal sage scrub. In some
places the fringed edges of its floodplain are 1.5 miles wide. This
basin gives birth to things. Some wildlife just winter here, nesting and procreating. Other wildlife live on base year round. The
endangered arroyo toad population in the lower Santa Margarita aspires to be a permanent resident: It's one of the core populations left in the United States, and possibly the world. The
small, stocky, warty toad may look tough, but it's actually in a
great deal of peril. According to the US Fish and Wildlife Service, when listed in 1994, only six of the twenty-two extant populations in the United States were known to contain more than
a dozen adult arroyo toads. As of 2014, most of the remaining
populations were still small, averaging ten to twelve breeding
adults in a given locality.

Long stretches of habitat near where the lower Santa Margarita meets De Luz Creek are thriving with native vegetation.
Located in Camp Pendleton's India training area, riverbanks
along here are shady willow, elderberry, cottonwood, sycamore,
and a tangled profusion of wild grape vine and blackberry
bush good for low-story coverage. Biologists Gwen Kenney and
Patrick McConnell help manage this part of the lower Santa
Margarita, work for Bieber, and are my guides for this stretch.

McConnell has the additional task of driving along the riparian corridor while calling in our coordinates to logistics HQ. Relatively new and not yet verbally proficient in military shorthand, McConnell reaches for the radio when Kenney informs him we had entered India a ways back.

"Long Rifle, Land Management, over," McConnell says, tentatively. Silence on the other end.

Kenney, who's McConnell's supervisor, speaks up helpfully from the backseat, "Give all your info—"

Before she can finish a crackly radio voice sounding impatient cuts her off: "Vehicles?"

McConnell fidgets with the buttons, pushes one, and says, "Yes. Land Management, 1969, three personnel, one vehicles." He takes his finger off the "talk" button, flustered. "Ugh. Plural. I pluralized vehicle...They can get so grumpy."

After a pause, the disembodied voice clears our transit through India, and McConnell returns his attention to the landscape and what he knows. He points to a mass of tall reeds, perhaps 20 feet high along the Santa Margarita. The plant looks like a mix of thick bamboo and dried cornstalk, packed so tightly together it presents a wall rather than a porous redoubt. "That's arundo. It's basically a habitat destroyer," McConnell says. Among those who study riparian habitats, arundo is considered the most serious pest plant in Southern California coastal rivers.

The giant reed arundo is an invasive exotic native to Eurasia and it can grow up to 2 inches a day. No one's sure exactly when it first appeared in the lower Santa Margarita, but it can be seen in the 1950 film *Sands of Iwo Jima*, filmed in part on Camp Pendleton. It has been an enemy to beat back since the base first began trying to control it. Surveys of the area during those early years found that the species occupied around 26 percent of the

Santa Margarita riparian system, or approximately 740 acres.

Kenney leads the invasives monitoring program for the base's three riparian drainages, the largest of which is the Santa Margarita. When she arrived on base in 2009, arundo eradication projects had been going on for more than twenty years. Her team's annual target, set by Bieber, is to help keep arundo and the two other most serious invasives—saltcedar (tamarisk) and the multistemmed herb perennial pepperweed—below 1 percent "occupancy." Since 2013, Kenney's team has hit between 1 and 3 percent. Kenney uses the geographical information system (GIS) to catalog locations and area measurements of invasive-species tracts, and the status of native-species recovery.

Key to riparian recovery is keeping these three space-hogging invasives out after their initial eradication, says McConnell. He has to continually come through and knock them back, he says. McConnell is the invasive-plant and habitat-restoration project manager. They are listed as two separate management roles, but really one cannot be done without the other. He's been at Camp Pendleton just over a year. While still in grad school fifteen years ago at San Diego State, he helped conduct long-term monitoring of arundo along the Santa Margarita at Camp Pendleton. "We had to cut through hundreds of yards of it when we did our transect back then. It's one of those plants that just doesn't let anything else exist within it," he says. Essentially, habitat restorers must go to war against the stuff and then create an environment healthy and resilient enough to thwart any new incursions.

Arundo does not replicate by producing and spreading its seeds but via its root mass or rhizome. I try to get McConnell to employ the analogy of zombies, which are by their nature really hard to kill, because that's what keeps coming to mind as he describes the lengths to which managers must go in order to keep the giant reed in check. He won't say "zombie," but he does explain that the arundo's eradication entails not just using heavy machinery to cut down and pulverize the plant stalk but also, critically, destroying its rhizome, usually buried under 3 to 10 feet of soil. Roots sprout not just from the rhizome but also from nodes spaced about 6 inches apart all along the myriad rootstalks. If you don't get that core root mass, it just keeps sprouting. The battle to keep arundo below the target of 1 percent occupancy in the lower Santa Margarita is ongoing, with no end in sight.

"Our crews cruise the entire drainage on a regular basis to keep invasives in low abundance. Otherwise they will continue to increase and hog up all the space," McConnell says. Arundo provides habitat for nonnative insects, and tends to form a barrier to, rather than shelter for, most other living things.

Both arundo and saltcedar gobble riparian habitat all the way to the water's edge, eating away at gently sloping riverbanks and the sandy, slow-moving shallows and pools where arroyo toads breed, and deposit and emerge from egg sacs. When water is channelized like that, it is transformed from a meandering and braided river into something with radically different dynamics. "I've seen areas where arundo was so thick the water cut 20 feet straight down, like a canyon. It's just arundo and then a steep drop-off," McConnell says. "If you've got no sandy habitat for the arroyo toad to breed and forage in, then you've got no arroyo toad." According to a 2011 report prepared by the California Invasive Plant Council, on a scale of one to ten, with one being "very low/improbable impact" and ten being "very severe impact," arundo scores an overall ten against the arroyo toad in the lower Santa Margarita.

To date, 1,300 acres of arundo and saltcedar have been removed from Camp Pendleton at a cost of around $10 million. The Defense Department does not track costs for treating invasive species on its lands, since there is no dedicated program, but during the same amount of time Camp Pendleton has been treating arundo—between roughly 1991 and 2016—the Defense Department spent $176.5 million to protect all the threatened or endangered plants on all the lands it controls.

Pendleton's treated acreage is recovering, as evidenced by the growth of native plants and trees and the increase in the endangered least Bell's vireo in the base's understory habitat. These delicate little songbirds of about 4.5 inches in length have short, rounded wings and are mostly gray above and pale below, a common protective covering that did not save its numbers from plummeting. The least Bell's vireo was listed as an endangered subspecies of the Bell's vireo in 1986. Recovery efforts have been ongoing since then for its few remaining populations—the majority located in California, with a smattering in Mexico—but the birds have failed to thrive most everywhere but along the Santa Margarita. According to the US Fish and Wildlife Service, which conducts five-year reviews on the status of threatened and endangered species, "Only the Camp Pendleton/Santa Margarita River and the Santa Ana River populations have clearly met the target of 'several hundred or more breeding pairs' of vireos at the designated site." The service added that these population increases "have likely been driven by habitat protection [and] habitat-quality improvement by the removal of invasive exotic plants."

"Gwen and I are both evangelists for plants. I've just been doing all the talking," says McConnell as we thrash through a thicket near the Santa Margarita. Kenney chimes in, "I'm not a talker. I'm a sit-at-my-desk, manage-my-contracts person," but the work, both in the office and in the wilds of Camp Pendleton, nourishes her, she says. Kenney's degree is in environmental and systematic biology from Cal Poly. Previous to Camp Pendleton, she was an environmental consultant but says of that role, "It was just sort of sucking out my soul. I went into the field because I love nature. Then you get a job in the environmental consulting world and every project you work on is a development project. It's either a landfill or a housing development or a building's going to be placed there. My job at Camp Pendleton is more in stewardship and taking care of the land."

McConnell points out black willows, sandbar willows, and what he calls false willows, then stops talking long enough to listen to the song of a least Bell's vireo hidden somewhere in the greenery. He's a plant guy after all, so as soon as the birdsong ends he nods toward a great leafy tree. "That's a populus...When you give natives a chance to spread, you create an ideal system for the animals and so forth. That's our goal: to try to get good cover, because whenever you have good cover, the invasives don't reach critical mass. They can't get to the light."

The recovery evidenced by the scene before us—one among the many tracts that Kenney monitors with GIS—has been preceded by an aggressive battle to reconquer altered habitat. Almost always, the eradication and management of invasives requires the application of herbicide. "Passive, without weed treatment? That was tried," says McConnell dismissively. "Especially in today's environment, where we continue to throw shocks to the natural system, we've got an altered riparian habitat that we have to actively manage."

In a nutshell, McConnell has just articulated the healthy-habitat paradox. Invasives are opportunistic and thrive in modified habitats, particularly ones in which native species have been compromised by climate change, disease, development, or unnaturally frequent fires. Tackling invasives without addressing their cause may seem like playing environmental whack-a-mole but, as in all of nature, altered habitat has a cascading and rarely salutary impact on the wider web of life. With some species on Camp Pendleton, fighting invasives is part of a race against extinction. The US Fish and Wildlife biological opinion for the base mandates that natural resources staff properly conserve and manage threatened and endangered species. To meet this requirement, managers must reverse engineer altered habitat. They must eradicate invasives before seeding the land with the kinds of native species that form the foundation of healthy habitat. After the heavy machinery come through to cut down and yank out as much of the arundo and saltcedar as possible, the root systems are doused with an herbicide containing glyphosate.

Glyphosate-based herbicides have been used since the 1970s and are today the most heavily applied herbicides in the world. As reported by the Royal Society of Chemistry, a 2016 scientific review of literature conducted by Myers Antoniou, Blumberg, et al. found that glyphosate remains in water and soil longer than thought, but how that translates to human and environmental risk remains unclear. "The risk of long-term, incremental buildup of glyphosate contamination in soil, surface water, and groundwater is therefore driven by highly site-specific factors, and as a result, is difficult to predict and costly to monitor," the scientists who conducted the review concluded. Based on the risk calculation of the state of California's scientists, however, in 2017 glysophate was added to the state's list. Monsanto, which produces the popular Roundup weed killer that contains glyphosate, is appealing the designation made by the state's Office of Environmental Health Hazard Assessment.

"Glyphosate and any kind of herbicide gets people uptight because they're still thinking in a Rachel Carson *Silent Spring*-kind of mentality," McConnell says. That would be me, I think. "But as a manager, you can't really take care of those invasives any other way, because they're so numerous and there's so much land to cover." McConnell had managed preserves in California for the Center for Natural Lands Management before coming to Camp Pendleton full time, he tells me, adding, "Any land manager will tell you that the number one threat to the biodiversity that they manage is invasive species."

Arundo is best treated in the fall before the first cold spell, when it's taken its first photosynthates—the sugars that give the plant its energy—back into its rhizome. By the time treatment begins, says McConnell, "the least Bell's vireo and basically most of your riparian songbirds have flown south." During bird breeding season, no one is allowed in this habitat at all, adds Kenney.

"And the arroyo toads are basically estivating when we're out here treating weeds. They're underground," McConnell says. "If we were hitting the arroyo toad with herbicides, the wildlife folks would be all over us! They'd find out. They'd know. They're really militant about their list of critters."

McConnell is referring to Sherri Sullivan, who did not strike me as at all militant. Higher-ups, including Bill Berry, Regional Conservation Program manager for Marine Corps Installations West, would also have something to say if McConnell killed off an endangered species on base.

BERRY AND CAMP PENDLETON'S chief game warden, Victor Yoder, are my guides into the rugged upland section of the Santa Margarita River. Berry is a big guy who looks intimidating but proves to be a cool customer, even when provoked—as I shortly discover. Yoder talks like someone who's worked for a government bureaucracy for a long time, which he has—between the two men, Berry and Yoder just about evenly split forty-five years' experience at Camp Pendleton—but I can easily imagine him wearing a goofy hunting cap, moving through tall grasses in pursuit of waterfowl. They both know the rules and follow them, and they both are committed to the conservation work they do.

Berry, who spends most of his time in an office now, says he didn't mind a bit when he was asked to drive up into the woodland backcountry of the Santa Margarita River drainage with a journalist. The view beyond our vehicle is of undeveloped expanses of majestic live oak, grassland, and chaparral.

Some of the training exercises occur in this rugged upland terrain. Ahead of us, a convoy of assault vehicles crawls up the road as we head into the Santa Margarita Mountains. Apparently not happy to see a civilian vehicle approach from behind, the marine in charge stands in the back of the last vehicle, glaring and gesturing sternly for Berry to slow down and back off.

"Okay. All right," Berry says while staring at the guy. "They may be expecting some kind of contact or something and they don't want me to get in the way." Thinking it would be best to extricate us from the training exercise, whatever it is, Berry decides to accelerate and pass all six vehicles in the convoy. It's the wrong call. The commanding marine appears to order his driver to accelerate after us. He then flags us to the side of the road, jumps out of his vehicle, and approaches the driver's side window, which Berry rolls down.

"I'm Lieutenant [X] with Bravo Company, from First LAR [light armored reconnaissance]," he says, angrily. "I want to be polite but I want to lose my shit on you for passing us. Do you understand how fucking...?" He stops, red-faced, then continues, "You were passing thirty-ton vehicles on a road that's had guys roll off it and die. And you're passing vehicles on blind curves with double yellow lines."

Berry, who looks to be at least twice the marine's age, lets a beat go by and then says in a measured voice, "Sir, I did not cross yellow lines or pass on a blind curve. I can guarantee you that. I understand your concern for the safety of your marines, absolutely, that comes first. I've worked on this installation twenty plus years. I take my job keeping you guys safe very seriously, so I'm not going to argue with you, other than to tell you I did what I did deliberately, consciously, and safely, with your safety and my safety in mind."

The exchange between the two men is tense, heightened by the fact that the convoy has stopped next to us in the road, (which does not seem at all safe), and the marines outside our vehicle are staring down at us, most of them holding high-powered assault rifles. For an instant on this isolated stretch I feel what it could be like to be confronted by American military might in the guise of young men, oozing testosterone and armed to the teeth, who are both scared and pissed off. It is not a good feeling.

The lieutenant doesn't accept Berry's explanation and keeps going, as though he needs to justify his aggressiveness by doubling down: "This road is possibly one of the most dangerous things for us that we traverse in our vehicles, and we've had a vehicle from the First LAR fall off it, and everyone died," he repeats.

After Berry apologizes, for perhaps the third time, we are allowed to move on. As he pulls back onto the road, he jokes, "I should have told him you were the general's wife!" Then he adds, "He's an officer, but he's a first lieutenant so he's pretty low on the food chain...What was he? Twenty-five? Twenty-six? Maybe that's the first time he's done this. He seemed very nervous. He could have stopped and we could have passed him and been out of his hair. But I guess he wanted the opportunity to get up in my face and yell at me." The altercation, mild as it was, has been a disquieting reminder that we are in a combat training zone with its own rules, weaponry, and hierarchies, and not just in an unpopulated, bucolic, California idyll (though it's that, too).

There are a few live-fire ranges and staging areas in this upland region but it's better suited to train foot patrols. The area doesn't really support large-scale vehicle maneuvers. As we had just witnessed, the vehicle travel is on the roads. "The training here is more, 'What's the best way to get through here?' You're not doing the marines any favors by clearing the trail network. They're going overseas. They're going to have to deal with terrain like this. They can't just bulldoze the terrain to make it easier to walk through. That's not training how they fight," says Berry. He points out rough foot trails on a nearby hillside. "The [noncommissioned officer] may say, 'Go over there and establish an observation point. The marines have to find their way, then set up their communications and cover-and-concealment-type things." Beyond the dirt road we are now on, and a few firebreak roads within sight, the landscape looks undisturbed and fairly impenetrable, so it's quite a surprise as we round a corner to see several marines pop out of the underbrush carrying compasses and maps.

We turn onto a washboard road and travel for a while along

a ridge that on one side slopes steeply toward the Santa Margarita River and on the other toward one of its tributaries, De Luz Creek. Camp Pendleton's southwest-northeast-trending drainages are positioned exactly right, so they're able to pull in moisture-laden marine air each day as land surfaces heat up. At night, the dry air is pulled down-canyon and seaward as the land surfaces cool. For all intents and purposes, it's more than a living landscape. The pristine lands along these drainages actually breathe.

This stretch of riparian corridor is part of the complicated circulatory system of the river and the region, joining coastal lowland to wooded upland, and connecting animals, amphibians, and birds to the fullness of their range.

"HEAR THAT?"

Alisa Zych stands still and cocks an ear toward the birdsong emanating from a nearby thicket. I've traveled off base with two Pendleton environmental managers and we are standing at a trailhead along the Santa Margarita River in the town of Fallbrook, just across the northeastern boundary of Camp Pendleton. The air is abuzz with insects, but the birdcall stands out.

. "Comefindme, comefindme, comefindme," Zych twitters, mimicking the sound. "That call, that up and down? That's the least Bell's vireo. It's chock-full of them in here."

This section of the Santa Margarita is tucked into more than 1,300 acres of undeveloped habitat currently owned by the Fallbrook Public Utility District. Zych and her colleague Kristin Thomas have brought me here to show how the Santa Margarita and its riparian habitat fare upstream from the base, and how choices made there can have deleterious effects downstream.

"This is kind of where the whole story begins," Zych says.

We form an easy trio, stopping for coffee along the way, small-talking about family and exercise regimes. They jog together in the hills around their Pendleton office during lunch and both clearly enjoy the opportunity their work affords to stomp around outdoors. They are added to my growing tally of women I've met on these military bases, most of whom are scientists and/or in environmental leadership positions. If the military hierarchy considers environmental security "women's work," and so gives many of the jobs to women, I'm thinking the joke is on the military because the women I've met are sharp. They're problem-solvers, multitaskers, and collaborators in a command-and-control environment, which perfectly fits the job requirements of ecosystem management.

The job also requires reaching across borders, which is why we are standing in the Santa Margarita preserve. Healthy habitat off base for threatened and endangered species helps reduce the chance that the base becomes a last refuge, which in turn increases the risk that training is impacted. Grounds can be taken out of circulation in order to protect those species and their new, adopted habitat.

Maintaining a "healthy tension" between the military mission on one end and the base's stewardship responsibilities on the other requires looking beyond the confines of the base itself and promoting healthy habitat there. It is complicated and ongoing work, says Jeff Paull, a former Marine Corps helicopter pilot with a Ph.D. from Princeton in environmental engineering. Paull's official title is Deputy Regional Director, Environmental Office, Military Installations West, Camp Pendleton. Basically, he's the guy in charge of the environmental security strategy, and it's his job to ensure that "healthy tension" does not devolve into zero-sum conflict. Stewardship beyond the base's boundaries and alliance-building with others to protect that habitat are essential strategies for protecting the military mission and therefore national security. Success here makes his job easier. "It's regional strategic work," Paull says, adding that his leadership team "works on that level to make sure their programs are not only satisfying the requirements today but are enduring for the future. We make long-term investments."

In 2017, while supporting a training tempo that has increased up to 27 percent in the last fifteen years, Paull's Natural Resources section was in the running for the top award for environmental restoration from the secretary of the navy. (Alas, it did not win.) None of this is exactly easy, but Camp Pendleton has proved that national security and natural security do not have to be mutually exclusive. They can coexist, and can do so all the more easily if regional ecosystem health is part of the mix. This enlightened self-interest was hard won, the result of exhausting confrontations between Camp Pendleton and its neighbors over the Santa Margarita River's precious natural resource.

Camp Pendleton had been a vast cattle ranch called the Rancho Santa Margarita y Las Flores when the Marine Corps acquired the ranch for $4.2 million in 1942. With that purchase, the military not only obtained land and shore critical for training combat forces but also partial water rights to the Santa Margarita River, which originates inland in the Santa Ana and Palomar Mountains.

The wrangling over the Santa Margarita's water has been both fierce and prolonged: A legal fight between downstream and upstream stakeholders over who controls it is among the longest-running civil cases in US history, in fact. The surprise is not that the waters of the Santa Margarita have been so relentlessly contested for nearly a century but that through it all the river and the riparian corridor it has carved over millennia have flourished. Even as the pressures of urban encroachment intensify upstream, the river has not been concreted over, deleteriously diverted, or sucked dry. It still makes it to the sea, and its banks still contain healthy stretches of every significant ecological zone historically occurring in Southern California. In demanding its share of the resource, Camp Pendleton has played a critical role in the Santa Margarita's overall health.

Others, of course, have not taken that view. One of them was the famous Hollywood director Frank Capra, a resident of Fallbrook, and perhaps Camp Pendleton's most well-known antagonist. Although the Korean War raged in 1952, the man behind *Mr. Smith Goes to Washington* and *It's a Wonderful Life* chose not to make a movie about American heroes or foreign threats that year but instead made *The Fallbrook Story*, a bizarre thirty-minute film that told the tale of how simple folks in the Southern California hamlet were being tyrannized by the United States government, operating on behalf of the nearby military base.

At issue, according to Capra's narrator, was "liberty and the dignity of the human soul." At issue, in fact, were water rights. An earlier state-court fight beginning in 1924 had granted the water to two large landholders, one of which was the Rancho Santa Margarita y Las Flores cattle ranch. Fearing that upstream population growth would suck up the precious resource before it reached the base, in 1951 the federal government sued to secure Camp Pendleton's continued access to a portion. Capra, who owned a large tract of productive farmland and definitely had a dog in the fight, was on the Fallbrook side of *United States v. Fallbrook Public Utility District* (he was also on the utility's board, according to the *San Diego Union Tribune*).

Shared water rights between Fallbrook and Camp Pendleton, which derives 95 percent of its groundwater supply from the Santa Margarita River basin, were decreed in a 1963 trial, but the judgment didn't solve the problem: Drought exacerbated by climate change has wreaked havoc on river flows, whose historic average formed the basis of the decree, while population in the upstream communities has grown exponentially since Capra's day. By 2020, that upper watershed area is expected to have at least twenty times the population size that existed in 1952. Reality overtook the decree. Although some legal tussles continue among other, lesser stakeholders, as a practical matter Camp Pendleton and the Fallbrook Public Utility District joined forces in 2001 and signed a binding memorandum of understanding to cooperatively and in good faith seek a "physical solution" to the legal dispute that had been dragging on between them for decades. The result was the Santa Margarita River Conjunctive Use Project, or CUP, as it's known. Where fighting failed, cooperation has made significant inroads in figuring out how to conserve and share a dwindling resource.

The CUP will never runneth over with water for any of its participants. The days of plenty in this arid, drought-prone, and intensively populated land are gone. But a good-faith effort between parties has borne mutually beneficial results: In November 2016, the US Navy agreed to a course of action developed by CUP that would finally gavel *United States v. Fallbrook Public Utility District* and bring the most long-running of the Santa Margarita's water fights to a close.

Zych and Thomas participated in the negotiations. "For the last five or six years, everybody has been on the same page. The team—from the base and from Fallbrook—is fantastic. It's a great group of people. We're all working in collaboration and moving forward," Thomas says.

Jack Bebee, acting general manager and chief engineer for the Fallbrook Public Utility District, agrees. He spent the last nine years as part of the negotiating team. "It was not an easy process. Fifty years were spent fighting over who got what water, but we finally did something instead of just fight. I think we developed a solution that protects all parties."

In addition to laying out a blueprint for new infrastructure that will improve the base's ability to recharge its groundwater while Fallbrook will get economically viable water projects, the deal also includes an agreement that the utility district permanently preserve all 1,392 acres of the habitat it owns along the Santa Margarita—the area "chock-full" of endangered least Bell's vireos, as Zych put it.

One conservation approach being considered for the new and permanent Santa Margarita preserve is what's called a perpetual conservation easement, which precludes development on the property in perpetuity. The Western Rivers Conservancy was in contracted negotiations to purchase and manage the preserve under such an easement agreement. Camp Pendleton, keen to make permanent the buffer zone created by the preserve, supported the conservancy's bid. More importantly, the base agreed to use funds from the Defense Department's Readiness and Environmental Protection Integration Program to help the conservancy purchase the land, whose market-value price tag is almost $10 million.

The base wanted a buffer zone against encroachment but it also wanted to ensure habitat protection for endangered species like the least Bell's vireo and the arroyo toad. Since both species are found on base as well, more room for them to roam relieves pressure on the installation. Part of the impetus is that this protected off-base habitat could be used as mitigation property by the base—in case it ever became necessary to expand training exercises into toad and vireo habitat on Camp Pendleton. Many consider this a loophole in Section 7 of the Endangered Species Act, because it allows a federal agency to bank conservation credits by restoring and conserving nonfederal land as a way to offset any future adverse effects to on-base listed species. I'm not keen on this escape valve because it has the power to let agencies off the conservation hook on their own properties. But, as far as I can tell, Camp Pendleton isn't shirking any on-base responsibilities while working toward this end.

Because both state- and federally listed species are found in the preserve, the US Fish and Wildlife Service as well as California's Department of Fish and Wildlife have also been involved in hammering out the particulars of sale. The negotiations were tough, but the parties finally came to an agreement. However, sealing the deal for good required extending the escrow, which in turn required a vote by the full board of the Fallbrook Public Utility District. At a raucous June 2017 public board meeting, the conservation easement deal with the Western Rivers Conservancy was voted down.

A group of recreationists including hikers and equestrians killed the conservation deal, a fact I found both astounding and shortsighted. Members of the Fallbrook Trails Council had long enjoyed hiking and riding in the preserve and did not like several components of the deal put forth by the state and federal wildlife agencies and strongly supported by Camp Pendleton and the conservancy. The first involved the *potential* closure of one stretch of an equestrian trail if any arroyo toads were found along it by conservation monitors during breeding season, which lasts about three months. The other sticking point related to trail maintenance. Historically, brush and weeds were cut back in the spring, when foliage grows to become a problem. That's breeding season for the least Bell's vireo, however, so the deal stated that trail clearing would occur in the fall instead. At the board meeting in Fallbrook, one recreationist after another rose to publicly denounce the deal, which was defeated in a three-to-two vote. Of note, Al Gebhart, the current president of the utility district, is a founding member of the Trails Council, and his wife is chair of that council and led the charge against the deal.

Peter Colby, California program director for the conservancy, was frustrated that long, hard negotiations had come to naught due to local opposition, but he praised Camp Pendleton's negotiators, particularly Thomas and Zych. "They approached this in a very pragmatic and rational way. They're good at protecting species, they're good environmental stewards, but they aren't nutso about it," Colby says. He's hopeful that his conservancy or another conservation group will ultimately work out a deal, with Camp Pendleton's financial support and scientific guidance. The deal's failure is disappointing, but the fact that a military installation was aligned with conservationists to create a permanent Santa Margarita River preserve is a hopeful sign.

"This [area] feeds into our watershed downstream, so its protection is key for Camp Pendleton. Invasive species move through this river. You get a high-flow event, and it just brings it all down," Zych says. She adds, "There are a lot of opportunities to restore this area. It's obviously beautiful, but we've got bullfrogs, we've got bats, we've got invasive fish all through here. We've got arundo and saltcedar."

Thomas agrees. Looking at the verdant and healthy habitat

along the banks of the river in the Santa Margarita preserve, Thomas says, "When I was first here ten years ago, the river was choked with arundo that [the base] helped clear out. We wouldn't have the native species as prolific as we have them if we hadn't been doing all that maintenance in the river. If it were still choked, you wouldn't have the birds."

Thomas is a civilian, and proud of the work she's done with the Marine Corps. Noting what a strange fact of modern life (and warfare) it is that 125,000 acres of relatively undisturbed land still exist along California's platinum coast—for military training—she adds: "The base has done a tremendous job of being a good steward of the environment. That's where it's a little bit tough, because I don't think we get enough recognition for all of the good deeds, just as our normal course of action. Outside base boundaries, stuff's gone."

In a world of competing and often hostile interests, one where environmental despoliation is occurring at a ravaging pace, it is instructive how effectively Camp Pendleton's stewards have been able to keep a steady eye on the key components of environmental security: Recover what's been damaged, encourage resilience, understand connections. In doing so there are myriad beneficial collateral effects—not least the proliferation of natural beauty, which has its own inherent healing effect.

ROBERT THIELEN IS living testimony of the salutary effects of natural beauty, coming home as he did a veteran with severe psychic scars. As he openly confessed during our visit, he'd seen too much and lost too much. He had been ravaged and hollowed out inside.

"There are no time-outs in combat," Thielen says. "I had a marine who killed somebody at a checkpoint. The person had failed to stop, so the marine was within his right of 'escalation of force.' But he still killed an innocent person, and he will have to deal with that for the rest of his life. During my tours of duty, I lost near fifty men and women I knew. I know the value of having the type of experience my facility offers prior to deployment. We're not going to save everybody, but I know it saves some."

One of the lives it has saved has been his own. Thielen returned from his fifth tour a mess. He didn't interact with others. He had no energy. He was tired all the time but couldn't sleep. His mind was a tangle of invasive thoughts he didn't want in there. He wasn't himself. "I wasn't in physical pain but..." he trails off.

Then, as luck would have it, he fell off a ladder. "I broke three ribs. The doctor gave me something for the pain..." I think I know where the story is headed, as most such stories do, but I'm wrong.

"Basically those pills knocked me out for five weeks. I got my sleep. When I felt better mentally I wanted to do more social activities. I started being more physical." One of Thielen's former commanding officers knew he was struggling and reached out. He suggested Thielen come aboard the base and help him run a new support center at Camp Pendleton: the Infantry Immersion Trainer. Thielen also wrote more poetry. One of those poems, "Foggy Perspective," captures the transformational link between peace of mind and a peaceful, beautiful environment. With hard-won clarity, the poet celebrates how a healthy natural world can in turn heal a wounded soul:

The morning's dew revealed by dawn,

reviving scent of plant and trees,

each breath of nature's nourishment

release a burdened spirit free.

The rhythmic step and crunch of leaves

upon the pebbly trodden way,

concedes the mind a just reprieve

in autumn's tranquil skies of grey.

Traverse the lane in migrant muse,

an aimless trek without a care;

while somewhere in the trees and hills,

once more, I've lost my troubles there.

EPILOGUE

The research, reporting, and writing of this book tracked fairly closely with the increasingly polarized 2016 US presidential campaign and its aftermath. It became more apparent as time passed that common ground was eroding. I remember thinking how, not so long ago, it was at least safe to talk about the weather among those you couldn't agree with about much else. With climate change consciously utilized as a campaign wedge issue, even the weather became too risky to talk about.

My reporting trips to military installations offered a surprising and welcome reprieve from counterfactual thinking: a place where climate change is an acknowledged threat multiplier; environmental decisions are made based on the law, science, and the will to exceed expectation; renewable energy is a sought-after component of energy security; and the rough sport of partisan politics is out of bounds.

To be sure, my survey was limited. Not all military facilities are led equally when it comes to stewardship and energy innovation, and some were easily crossed off the list early on. I can only report on those I visited and the people with whom I interacted.

The military may be rigid, primed for violence, and inherently conservative, but it is also by necessity both tactical and strategic; it must plan for future contingencies and then figure out how to execute. On the installations I visited, the overlay of environmental law with the geopolitical instability posed by a dependence on fossil fuels drives much of what is good about their energy and environmental initiatives. They are showing the way forward even as other military installations, and government agencies created to protect public health and the environment, falter.

This is not a conclusion I expected to reach—that the Department of Defense could be a standard bearer for how to create a sustainable twenty-first-century energy infrastructure or how to practice protection and stewardship of our natural and cultural patrimony. That the military is increasingly important to the future of biodiversity in California and elsewhere? I believe that now because I have witnessed how a more comprehensive notion of defense can and does work on the ground.

It's a hopeful sign that the US Department of Defense provides a refuge for level-headed thinking and leadership on matters of sustainability and ecological threat. It clearly possesses the discipline, decision-making structure, and resources to get things done. I only hope that in writing this book I haven't put a target on its innovative and much-needed projects.

NOTES

Please visit https://heydaybooks.com/unlikely-ally-notes for a version of these endnotes with live links to websites.

PREFACE

ix   Arizona Public Service: The author's father, Richard Berlin Snell, was on the APS board of directors from 1975 to 1999; from 1990 to 1999 he was chair, president, and CEO of Pinnacle West. APS is Pinnacle's largest subsidiary. It was exceedingly helpful to get this utility industry veteran's perspective on the current state of affairs in California.

xi   The authors of a 2017 paper for the Truman Center: Andreas Mueller, Peter Liebert, and Austin Heyworth, *Keeping the Lights On: The Critical Role of U.S. States in Electrical Sector Cybersecurity*, Truman Center, April 2017.

xi   "Unleash us from the tether of fuel": *Future Fuels*, Naval Research Advisory Committee Report, April 2006. General James Mattis expanded upon this statement during a hearing on the National Defense Authorization Act of 2012. When asked what he meant by his earlier call that the US military must be freed from its dependence on fossil fuels, he replied:

"[I]t is a significant Achilles heel for us when you have to haul the amounts of fuel that we have to haul around the battlefield for the generators and for the vehicles. We are working with DARPA [Defense Advanced Research Projects Agency]; we are working with a number of civilian organizations to try and find solutions. There are efforts under way to make more expeditionary bases which would actually generate some of their own energy requirements using, for example, solar power. In many of these places, there is a lot of sunshine. If we can get expeditionary capability to capture that and then basically recharge our batteries. I mean, it is an amazingly complex effort to maintain the fuel lines. And it also gives the enemy an ability to choose the time and place of attacking us. We are engaged with Science and Technology, we are engaged with DARPA, and we are looking at very pragmatic ways of doing this."

xiii The commandant of the Marine Corps had identified energy as a top priority: United States Marine Corps Expeditionary Energy Strategy and Implementation Plan: *Bases-to-Battlefield*, James F. Amos, general, US Marine Corps, commandant of the Marine Corps, p. 21 and Annex B. Specifically, the plan states: "Our approach to installation energy will achieve legislative, executive, and Secretary of the Navy mandates for reduced energy and water consumption and increased use of alternative energy. Through the combination of on-installation alternative energy production and energy demand reduction, 50 percent of our bases and stations will be net-zero energy consumers by 2020." I used the term "renewable" without an exact percentage goal in order to exclude nuclear power from the mix.

xv California Assembly Bill (AB) 327 (2013): See in particular Sec. 9 Sec. 2827 (4), which defines "eligible customer-generator." Sec. 11 Sec. 2827.1 (a) says that the new tariff must use the same definition of "eligible customer-generator" as in 2827; 2827.1 (5) says that the California Public Utilities Commission can allow systems larger than 1 megawatt, capped only by on-site load; and 2827.1 (6) set up a new rulemaking (R.14-07-002) to implement the new law. https://leginfo.legislature.ca.gov/faces/billVersionsCompareClient.xhtml?bill_id=201320140AB327.

xvi Electric Rule 21: Early on, I mistakenly thought that Rule 21 was the cause of the limits on how much renewable energy could be generated on military installations in California; it is, rather, the effect (or marching orders) based on legislation and PUC rulemaking R.14-07-002 below. Rule 21 is "a tariff that describes the interconnection, operating and metering requirements for generation facilities to be connected to a utility's distribution system." http://www.cpuc.ca.gov/Rule21.

xvii   Set up its rulemaking schedule (R.14-07-002): http://www.cpuc.ca.gov/General.aspx?id=3934.

xvii   The Public Utilities Commission issued its new net energy metering rules (D.16-01-044): This 2016 decision kept net metering and ruled that systems could be any size as long as they were intended to offset on-site load. However, it limited military bases to the 12-megawatt cap from SB 83. See Sec. 2.14.4.2 of "Customer Generators Eligible Under SB 83," pp. 97–8: http://docs.cpuc.ca.gov/PublishedDocs/Published/G000/M158/K181/158181678.pdf.

xix   Senate Bill (SB) 83 (2015): Sec. 39 (a–m) of this bill is a fascinating exercise in misdirection. The real show starts at Sec. 40 (4)(c)(i–iv): https://leginfo.legislature.ca.gov/faces/billTextClient.xhtml?bill_id=201520160SB83.

xxi   Budget trailer bills: They are an unintended consequence of a 1987 California State Supreme Court ruling in *Harbor v. Deukmejian*: https://law.justia.com/cases/california/supreme-court/3d/43/1078.html; Proposition 25, passed in 2010, has also played a role: http://www.lao.ca.gov/ballot/2010/25_11_2010.aspx.

For further reading: *The Grid: The Fraying Wires between Americans and Our Energy Future*, by Gretchen Bakke (New York: Bloomsbury, 2016).

INTRODUCTION

xxix   The US military is the planet's dominant war-fighting machine: Country data comes from the Stockholm International Peace Research Institute (SIPRI), April 24, 2017. It delineates respective "military expenditures," a term that includes spending on "current military forces and activities, including salaries and benefits, operational expenses, arms and equipment purchases, military construction, research and development, and central administration, command and support."

xxix   Profile of Major General Michael Lehnert of the Marine Corps: "A Few Good Species," by Marilyn Berlin Snell, *Sierra* (November/December 2006). https://www.marilynberlinsnell.com/ND06-Profile-Lehnert.pdf.

xxxi   French Impressionist painters traveled to the front: Appreciating the war effort in its many guises (and disguises): *Disruptive Pattern Material: An Encyclopedia of Camouflage*, by Hardy Blechman (Richmond Hill, Ontario: Firefly Books, 2004), p. 129.

xxxi   The first "frog-skin" camouflage: The war and peace exercises in visual subterfuge are beautifully rendered and explained in *Camouflage*, by Tim Newark and Jonathan Miller (London: Thames & Hudson, 2007), p. 130.

xxxii   The 2004 National Defense Authorization Act: Specifically Sec. 318 of HR 1588—National Defense Authorization Act for Fiscal Year 2004 at https://www.congress.gov/bill/108th-congress/house-bill/1588/text. For a helpful analysis of critical habitat exemptions: "An Evaluation of Endangered Species Act Exemptions in the Department of Defense and the U.S. Air Force," by Charles A. Bleckmann, Ellen C. England, and E. Sitzabee, *Federal Facilities Environmental Journal* 15, no. 3 (September 2004), pp. 19–28. http://onlinelibrary.wiley.com/doi/10.1002/ffej.20021/abstract.

xxxiii   The world is carried through the universe on a turtle's back: There are surprising similarities between some indigenous North American tribes' stories and Asiatic (particularly Indian) stories about the earth being supported on the back of a floating tortoise. See *Researches into the Early History of Mankind and the Development of Civilization*, by Edward Burnett Tylor (Boston: Estes & Lauriat, 1878), pp. 342–44.

xxxv   In *The Art of War*: *The Art of War: Complete Texts and Commentaries*, by Sun Tzu (Boulder, CO: Shambhala Publications, 2005), p. 6.

CHAPTER 1

5 Army Net Zero Initiative: In 2010 Assistant Secretary of the Army for Installations, Energy, and Environment Katherine Hammack announced the initiative: "The primary goal is a focus toward net zero, and when we talk about net zero, it's not only net zero energy, but it's net zero energy, water, and waste. When you look at the term 'net zero' or a hierarchy of net zero you must start with reduction, then progress through repurposing, recycling, energy recovery, disposal being the last." http://www.asaie.army.mil/Public/IE/doc/Net%20Zero%20White%20Paper%20V2.pdf.

6 Legislation passed in 1976: The Resource Conservation and Recovery Act gave the Environmental Protection Agency the authority to control hazardous waste "from cradle to grave." https://www.epa.gov/laws-regulations/summary-resource-conservation-and-recovery-act.

6 The *New York Times* reported in 1991: "Toxic Pollution at Military Sites Is Posing a Crisis," by Keith Schneider, June 30, 1991, is a sober reminder of the important role civil society plays in holding the military accountable.

7 More recent investigative reporting: ProPublica's Abrahm Lustgarten updates Schneider's work in the series, Bombs in Our Backyard, a series of reports that began July 20, 2017, with "Open Burns, Ill Winds." https://www.propublica.org/series/bombs-in-our-backyard.

7 Fort Irwin, too, has a legacy of profligate burning and disposal of hazardous material: The National Training Center and Fort Irwin fiscal year 2016 Army Defense Environmental Restoration Program Installation Plan chronicles the toxic legacy of the base. "Forty-four sites are currently listed in the Army Environmental Database-Restoration (AEDB-R) for NTC and Fort Irwin; only three sites are still active and are all in long-term management."

10 **The federal Budget Control Act of 2011**: A helpful explanation of the act's effects: "How the Across-the-Board Cuts in the Budget Control Act Will Work," by Richard Kogan for the Center on Budget and Policy Priorities, revised April 27, 2012. https://www.cbpp.org/research/how-the-across-the-board-cuts-in-the-budget-control-act-will-work.

11 **A bioremediation process similar to that used after the Deepwater Horizon oil spill**: A good primer on how the process works: "Oil Biodegradation and Bioremediation: A Tale of the Two Worst Spills in US History," by Ronald M. Atlas, *Environmental Science & Technology* 45, no. 16 (August 15, 2011). https://www.ncbi.nlm.nih.gov/pmc/articles/PMC3155281.

12 **Energy Savings Performance Contract**: The contracts are a great idea and are supposed to work like this: https://energy.gov/eere/femp/energy-savings-performance-contracts-federal-agencies. The Government Accountability Office reviewed the program and determined the contracts did not always live up to their promise: "Energy Savings Performance Contracts: Additional Actions Needed to Improve Federal Oversight," GAO-15-432, June 17, 2015. https://www.gao.gov/products/GAO-15-432.

12 **According to the Federal Energy Management Program**: The Senate Committee on Energy and Natural Resources was keen to increase the use of performance contracting because it saw the benefits of energy efficiency efforts in conserving domestic resources and saving American consumers money. See S. Rpt. 115-79 "Energy Savings through Public-Private Partnerships Act of 2017," 115th Congress (2017–18): https://www.congress.gov/congressional-report/115th-congress/senate-report/79/1.

14 **Clean Air Act permits**: According to Fort Irwin's chief of the Environmental Division of public works, Justine Dishart, the facility's emissions did not trigger Title V permit requirements under the Clean Air Act, which can be found at https://www.epa.gov/title-v-operating-permits.

17   Bertram filed a lawsuit in September 2015: The court battle between Integrated Energy LLC and Siemens Government Technologies is Case No. 8:15-cv-01534-JVS-DFM, United States District Court, Central District of California, Southern Division, James V. Selna presiding. Bertram first filed her complaint on September 23, 2015. As of December 22, 2017, when the case history was accessed on PACER (Public Access to Court Electronic Records: https://www.pacer.gov), the legal fight continues.

20   General James Mattis noted: Thanks to ProPublica for making the previously unpublished transcript available: https://www.documentcloud.org/documents/3518910-MattisResponsestoQFRs-MASTERCOPY.html.

21   The base's new $211 million super-green hospital: The Weed Army Community Hospital provides soldier and family patient care and is a model for how beautiful sustainable design can be. See also, "Building the World's 'Greenest' Hospital," by Major Jeffrey M. Beeman, *The Military Engineer* 108, no. 705 (November–December 2016), p. 50.

CHAPTER 2

29   In the first seven months of 1942: The New England Historical Society has a bracing account (http://www.newenglandhistoricalsociety.com/u-boat-attacks-of-world-war-ii-6-months-of-secret-terror-in-the-atlantic), as does a recounting of the U-boat offensive *Antisubmarine Warfare in World War II*, by Charles M. Sternhell and Alan M. Thorndike, produced by the Operations Evaluation Group, Office of the Chief of Naval Operations (Washington, D.C., 1946), report no. 51, p. 25: http://www.ibiblio.org/hyperwar/USN/rep/ASW-51/.

29   The navy contracted with the California Institute of Technology: The history of China Lake is fascinating, and well told in the documentary *Secret City: A History of the Navy at China Lake*, produced by the China Lake Museum Foundation to celebrate the installation's fiftieth anniversary.

29 **Huge booms in the middle of the night when something blew up**: A great oral history of Victor V. Veysey, who joined the staff of Caltech's newly established Industrial Relations Center (IRC) in 1939, and who was interviewed about his experiences in 1993 and 1994, tells the story of the early years. From the archives of Caltech: http://oralhistories.library.caltech.edu/105/1/OHO_Veysey_V.pdf; see particularly p. 10.

34 **One patented process utilizes resveratrol**: What's not to like about a compound that holds out the promise of preventing and/or treating everything from cancer to cardiovascular and neuro-degenerative diseases? See the Mayo Clinic's article "Red Wine and Resveratrol: Good for Your Heart?" at https://www.mayoclinic.org/diseases-conditions/heart-disease/in-depth/red-wine/art-20048281?pg=2 and "Resveratrol and Cancer: Focus on *In Vivo* Evidence," by Lindsay G. Carter, John A. D'Orazio, and Kevin J. Pearson, *Endocrine-Related Cancer* 21, no. 3 (June 2014): https://www.ncbi.nlm.nih.gov/pmc/articles/PMC4013237.

35 **Methylenedianiline...is carcinogenic and mutagenic**: The planet will benefit when a replacement for this nasty compound comes into widespread use. See the Agency for Toxic Substances and Disease Registry: https://www.atsdr.cdc.gov/toxfaqs/tf.asp?id=1000&tid=210. Employee exposure is regulated by OSHA at ten parts per billion over an eight-hour day: https://www.osha.gov/pls/oshaweb/owadisp.show_document?p_table=standards&p_id=10081.

36 ***Buck Rogers in the 25th Century: An Interplanetary Battle with the Tiger Men of Mars***: In some ways, we have come so very far. In others, not nearly far enough. This brief film made in 1934 reveals a poignant moment on the American trajectory of technological progress: https://www.youtube.com/watch?v=qm4I8B3b-FUA.

40 **Along the eastern "shoreline" of China Lake**: Mark A. Giambastiani and Thomas Bullard's fascinating look at the paleohydrology of China Lake during the late Pleistocene epoch reveals that the area was once part of the vast Owens River drainage system of seven interconnected lakes that extended hundreds of linear miles. "Terminal Pleistocine: Early Holocene Occupations on the Eastern Shoreline of China Lake, California," *Pacific Coast Archaeological Society Quarterly* 43, nos. 1 and 2 (2007), pp. 51–52. http://pcas.org/assets/documents/5.TerminalPleistocene-earlyHoloceneOccupations.pdf.

40 According to anthropologist Emma Lou Davis: "The 'Exposed Archaeology' of China Lake, California," *American Antiquity* 40, no. 1 (January 1975), pp. 39–53. Davis was an early supporter of military cultural stewardship: "Thanks entirely to the fact that the China Lake valley has been a naval bombing range for [more than] 25 years, deposits of artifacts and of faunal remains have not been significantly disturbed. The archaeology and paleontology of a wide area are protected from vandals, and lie where they have been for centuries and millennia—slowly weathering out from beneath sandy lacustrine mantles left by a last high lake level. The educational value of such a study area is immense and it is almost unique as an environmental resource of a kind which elsewhere is being recklessly squandered by bulldozing, building, and pilfering 'collections.'" Her archives, the E. L. Davis Collection, are housed in the San Diego Museum of Man. https://www.jstor.org/stable/279267?seq=1#page_scan_tab_contents. Davis referred to the petroglyph canyons of China Lake as "message headquarters."

42 Contractors working with the navy have nearly completed a 3-D virtual tour: The work in progress, by PaleoWest Archaeology, is worth a preview: https://core.tdar.org/document/429658/3d-modeling-and-virtual-reality-for-condition-assessments-and-educational-outreach-tools-documenting-rock-art-in-little-petroglyph-canyon-naval-air-weapons-station-china-lake-california and https://sketchfab.com/models/03b269a91e4642338d1805b6acfd1111.

43 There is no consensus among archaeologists: The Maturango Museum in Ridgecrest is a good resource for archaeological work done in the Coso Range: https://maturango.org.

45 *Talking Stone: Rock Art of the Cosos*: For those who can't see the rock art in situ, this is a fine introduction. It was produced, directed, and filmed by Paul Goldsmith, 2014, the Bradshaw Foundation.

45   The Coso Geothermal Field is one of the largest producers of geothermal electricity in the country: In the deal that transferred ownership of the Coso geothermal project to Southern California Edison in 1985, under a thirty-year contract, all of the power goes onto the local utility grid. Had Naval Air Weapons Station China Lake been cut into the power-purchase deal, it would be completely energy independent today (see Appendix J: https://www.sce.com/NR/sc3/tm2/pdf/3330-E.pdf).

46   In a 2002 Senate hearing on sacred places: *Hearing before the Committee on Indian Affairs on the Protection of Native American Sacred Places as They Are Affected by Department of Defense Undertakings*, 107th Congress, second session on June 4, 2002 (statement of Rachel A. Joseph, chairperson, Lone Pine Paiute-Shoshone Tribe, Lone Pine, CA). https://www.gpo.gov/fdsys/pkg/CHRG-107shrg80363/html/CHRG-107shrg80363.htm.

46   Instead, later that year the Department of Energy awarded $4.5 million: According to a *Geothermal Energy Status Report* funded by the European Commission in 2015, the fracking feasibility study was stopped after a large natural fracture was encountered during the deepening of one of the wells. For the initial project description see: "Enhanced Geothermal Systems Project Development—Phase Three," https://energy.gov/eere/geothermal/awards-archive.

47   According to researchers at MIT's Department of Aeronautics and Astronautics: "A Link Between Air Travel and Deaths on the Ground," by Morgan Bettex, *MIT News*, September 28, 2010. http://news.mit.edu/2010/airplane-emissions-0928.

CHAPTER 3

49   Brown is still out front: When Governor Brown signed SB 32 in 2016, he strengthened the state's greenhouse gas emission reduction goals, which were already the most ambitious in the United

States. He also signed AB 197, which requires California to cut emissions at least 40 percent below 1990 levels by 2030 and invest in the communities hardest hit by climate change (https://www.gov.ca.gov/news.php?id=19522). In advance of the United Nations Climate Change Conference in Paris, Governor Brown signed the Under2 MOU (http://under2mou.org), a first-of-its-kind agreement between states and provinces around the world to limit the increase in global average temperatures to below 2 degrees Celsius (https://www.gov.ca.gov/docs/Under_2_MOU.pdf). In July 2017, Brown and former New York City mayor Michael Bloomberg launched an initiative to compile and quantify the actions of states, cities, and businesses in the United States to help drive down their greenhouse gas emissions consistent with the Paris Agreement goals (https://www.gov.ca.gov/news.php?id=19872). In September 2018 Governor Brown will convene the Global Climate Action Summit in San Francisco (https://globalclimateactionsummit.org).

50   **The sense of urgency is well founded:** Climate scientist Daniel Swain's *California Weather Blog* provides a deep dive into the science and implications of current California weather patterns: http://weatherwest.com.

50   **The California Department of Water Resources warns that climate change is having a "profound" impact on California:** By the end of this century, the Sierra snowpack is projected to experience a 48 to 65 percent loss from the historical April 1 average, which means there will be a lot less water available for Californians: https://www.water.ca.gov/Programs/All-Programs/Climate-Change-Program.

52   **Crossing the Dust Bowl region of West Texas in 1932:** This silent film from the National Film Preservation Foundation captures the christening scene of the USS *Akron*: https://www.youtube.com/watch?v=ZjPqK8dYD1A. Warning: This disturbing bit of film, "Akron Accident San Diego May 11th 1932," captures the scene when three sailors let go of the lines connecting them to the ascending airship: https://www.youtube.com/watch?v=Y_kSNWMeFXE.

57   Environmental Security Technology Certification Program: The ESTCP was founded in 1995 to promote innovative and cost-effective technology transfer: https://www.serdp-estcp.org/About-SERDP-and-ESTCP/About-ESTCP. More information about Raytheon's bid to improve energy resiliency at Miramar with a building-capacity microgrid can be found at https://www.serdp-estcp.org/News-and-Events/Blog/Improving-Energy-Security-and-Resilience-of-DoD-Installations/(language)/eng-US.

59   Each year, more than 900,000 tons of trash come through Miramar Landfill's gates: A succinct primer on goals and accomplishments can be found at https://www.epa.gov/sites/production/files/2016-05/documents/27_purtee.pdf.

60   Methane—straight out of the ground: You can read more about why methane is more potent than carbon dioxide as a greenhouse gas on the EPA's website: https://www.epa.gov/ghgemissions/understanding-global-warming-potentials. The Intergovernmental Panel on Climate Change has this to say about methane: https://www.ipcc.ch/publications_and_data/ar4/wg1/en/ch2s2-3-2.html.

61   Miramar Landfill and San Diego Metro Biosolids Center: Who knew trash and sewage could be so productive? The Cogeneration Channel produced a short video about the project entitled *Cogeneration from Landfill and Waste Water: Two Success Stories in San Diego*: www.cogenerationchannel.com/en/video/category/biogas-e-biomasse/605/cogenerazione-da-discarica-e-acque-re-flue-due-casi.

62   Pure Water project: Where federal infrastructure projects fail to materialize, cities are doing it for themselves: https://www.san-diego.gov/water/purewater/purewatersd.

66   Miramar and all other military installations in California are currently restricted by law and Public Utilities Commission regulations from exporting excess power back onto the grid: Yes, I've already mentioned this elsewhere. Yes, it's a problem and needs to be addressed: https://leginfo.legislature.ca.gov/faces/billTextClient.xhtml?bill_id=201520160SB83. SB 83 Sec. 40: Sec. 2827 of the PUC code is amended at 4(c)(ii) and (iii).

66 But what if Miramar were allowed to provide power to the grid when it was really needed...and be paid a fair price for it in the form of what's called a feed-in tariff: California currently has a renewable feed-in tariff program, but military installations are unable to take advantage of it and, as is, the program is limited to small renewable generators less than 3 megawatts in size: http://www.cpuc.ca.gov/feedintariff.

68 SDG&E had a successful demonstration 4.6-megawatt microgrid project: *Borrego Springs Microgrid Demonstration Project*, Final Project Report prepared for the California Energy Commission by San Diego Gas & Electric and the Horizon Energy Group, October 2013: http://www.energy.ca.gov/2014publications/CEC-500-2014-067/CEC-500-2014-067.pdf. From SDG&E's website: "Microgrids: Small but Mighty," September 5, 2017, http://sdgenews.com/reliable/microgrids-small-mighty.

CHAPTER 4

71 By every substantive legal measure: In *Winter v. Natural Resources Defense Council, Inc.*, plaintiffs sought relief on the grounds that the navy's training exercises violated the National Environmental Policy Act of 1969 and other federal laws. The US Supreme Court decision of November 12, 2008, did not address the merits of the case but instead sidestepped them completely to hold that: "The balance of equities and the public interest—which were barely addressed by the District Court—tip strongly in favor of the Navy. The Navy's need to conduct realistic training with active sonar to respond to the threat posed by enemy submarines plainly outweighs the interests advanced by the plaintiffs." For a full rundown on the various court rulings that led to this decision see https://www.supremecourt.gov/opinions/08pdf/07-1239.pdf.

72 Hitler was also utilizing a new technology: A refresher course on the dangers of despots and falsified news: *Propaganda and the Ethics of Persuasion*, 2nd ed., by Randal Marlin (Buffalo, NY: Broadview Press, 2013), p. 79.

75 **FBI documents chronicling the surveillance**: There were actually between "40 and 60 FBI reports of Earth Day rallies on April 22, 1971," according to Senator Muskie's congressional statement. Rhetorically, he asks: "If antipollution rallies are a subject of intelligence concern, is anything immune?" See http://abacus.bates.edu/muskie-archives/ajcr/1971/FBI%20Speech.shtml.

80 **Radiocarbon samples**: "Overview of the Archaeology of San Clemente Island, California," by Clement W. Meighan, *Pacific Coast Archaeological Society Quarterly* 36, no. 1 (Winter 2000), p. 5. http://www.pcas.org/vol36n1/1meighan.pdf.

80 **They even utilized a "Judas" goat**: Dastardly perhaps, but effective: "Feral Goat Eradication on San Clemente Island, California," by Dawn R. Keegan, Bruce E. Coblentz, and Clark S. Winchell., *Wildlife Society Bulletin* 22, no. 1 (Spring 1994), pp. 56–61.

81 **Learning how to revivify a land laid waste by unchecked ungulates**: "Spreading Deserts: The Hand of Man," by Erik Eckholm and Lester R. Brown, *Bulletin of the Atomic Scientists* (January 1978), pp. 10–16. Yet, lack of water is an ever-increasing threat as well. See *The Role of Water Stress in Instability and Conflict*, December 2017, published by CNA: https://www.cna.org/CNA_files/PDF/CRM-2017-U-016532-Final.pdf.

84 **When ornithologists first sighted the San Clemente Island Bell's sparrow**: C. B. Linton documents an early sighting in "Notes from San Clemente Island," *The Condor* 10, no. 2 (March–April 1908), p. 85, published by the American Ornithological Society, "*Amphispiza belli*. Bell Sparrow. Common resident on the brushy portions of the northwest half of the Island."

90 **The National Defense Authorization Act passed that year (2004)**: Sec. 319 "amends the Marine Mammal Protection Act of 1972 to add the definition of 'harassment' with respect to a military readiness activity[;] authorizes the Secretary, after conferring with the Secretary of Commerce or the Interior (or both), to exempt any action or category of actions undertaken by DoD or its components from compliance with any requirement of such Act if the

Secretary determines that the exemption is necessary for national defense[; and] allows the incidental takings of marine mammals while engaged in a military readiness activity requiring publication of notice thereof only in the Federal Register.

90 Research has shown that the loud noises emitted via mid-frequency active sonar: Two pioneering studies published in 2013 offered the first direct measurements of whales' responses to mid-frequency active military sonar. Both issued from the Southern California Behavioral Response Study, a multiyear interdisciplinary study led by two of the United States' leading experts on underwater noise pollution, and substantially funded by the navy: "Blue Whales Respond to Simulated Mid-frequency Military Sonar," by Jeremy A. Goldbogen, Brandon L. Southall, Stacy L. DeRuiter, et al., *Proceedings of the Royal Society B*, 280, no. 1785 (August 22, 2013); and "First Direct Measurements of Behavioural Responses by Cuvier's Beaked Whales to Mid-frequency Active Sonar," by Stacy L. DeRuiter, Brandon L. Southall, John Calambokidis, et al., *Biology Letters* 9, no. 4 (July 3, 2013). Both are published by Royal Society Publishing.

92 The studies have also revealed insights: The Office of Naval Research has funded studies that look into how prolonged exposure to stressors like sound may result in immune system suppression, reproductive failure, accelerated aging, and slowed growth in marine mammals; technology funded in part by the navy passively detects and automatically classifies marine mammal vocalizations to help the navy and commercial shipping concerns avoid marine mammals and mitigate harm. The study of echolocation in marine mammals has led to the field of bioacoustics, a combination of acoustics and biology. Though still in its infancy, scientists are hoping that it will improve our ability to detect human diseases in their early stages.

93 During the run-up to and early months of the Iraq War: See especially the testimony of March 13 and April 1, 2003, before the Committee on Armed Services, United States Senate, 108th Congress, *Impacts of Environmental Laws on Readiness and the Related Administration Legislative Proposal*; and the statement of Rear

Admiral Robert T. Moeller, US Navy deputy chief of staff for operations, before the House Committee on Resources, May 6, 2003: http://
www.navy.mil/navydata/testimony/readiness/moeller030506
.txt.

For further reading: *War of the Whales: A True Story*, by Joshua
Horwitz (New York: Simon & Schuster, 2014).

CHAPTER 5

98   North of town is more crew cut: New male recruits' heads are
shaved, but as they progress through the rigors of the Marine Corps
they are able to work the slightest bit of individuality into hairstyles:
They can stay shaved or don a high-and-tight, or a high, medium, or
low fade, et cetera. I was unable to determine why marines are not
allowed to part their hair down the middle.

99   If successful, it will become a planned "desire path": Epi-
sode 263 of the podcast *99% Invisible* by Roman Mars explores
the meaning of desire paths, which are, as *99% Invisible* figures it,
"unplanned routes that people just really want to take." Animals
exhibit the same kind of behavior. Shaped by repeated use, desire
paths are found everywhere—from rough dirt trails on remote hill-
sides to paths through grass in urban parks. Mostly, desire paths
are shortcuts, but they can also be "long cuts"—as when sojourn-
ers want to stay on the neutral side of superstition. Urban planners
often try to foresee desire paths, and then design either to facilitate
them or to subtly manipulate behavior and flow; the same principle
holds for the designers of wildlife corridors.

**99   Several key sections of the law fulfilled the wish of the Marine
Corps**: The Marine Corps issued its *Operational Training Ranges
Required Capabilities* document in June 2006: http://www.marines.
mil/Portals/59/MCRP%203-0C%20z.pdf.

**99   It may also have changed the survival prospects for *Gopherus
agassizii***: The tortoise was given its Latin name by James Graham Cooper. A surgeon by trade and a naturalist by family tree
and vocation (the Cooper's hawk is named for his father), Cooper

signed up for adventure as a physician with the army in 1860 so he could roam the landscape and survey the skies. The army abandoned Fort Mohave on May 28, 1861, so that troops could be sent east to fight the American Civil War, but not before Cooper became the first Caucasian to note two news birds—a warbler and an owl—and a tortoise. He wrote to his friend (and assistant secretary of the Smithsonian Institution) Spencer Baird that he was naming the warbler after Baird's daughter Lucy, then added: "I intend to call the owl *Whitneyi* [after geologist Josiah Whitney]....It will be a better compliment than to name the tortoise after him, the bird of wisdom instead of the emblem of slowness—who shall I name *it* for, Agassiz?" Cooper did in fact name the desert tortoise *Gopherus agassizii*, after Swiss American biologist and geologist Louis Agassiz. It remains unclear, however, whether Cooper's linking of slowness to Agassiz was in reference to the latter's work on glaciology or to his retrograde resistance to the theory of Darwinian evolution. From, *James Graham Cooper: Pioneer Western Naturalist*, by Eugene V. Coan (Moscow, ID: Idaho Research Foundation, 1982); and "A Sketch" by W. O. Emerson, *Bulletin of the Cooper Ornithological Club* 1, no. 1 (January–February 1899).

100 The majority of the base likely looks much as it did: The Chemehuevi are the southernmost branch of the Southern Paiute people. In 1853, the federal government declared the Chemehuevi's land to be public domain and later relocated the Chemehuevi to what is now called the Colorado River Indian Reservation. During World War II, the federal government established the Japanese concentration camp Poston. The Serrano people ranged throughout the area now occupied by the combat center. After a revolt against settlers and missionaries in 1810, many were forcibly moved to Mission San Gabriel; others later found refuge on what became the Morongo Indian Reservation.

101 It spends a lot of time in that burrow: The US Fish and Wildlife Service refers to the Mojave Desert tortoise as "one of the most elusive inhabitants of the desert"—in part because their populations have been decimated, but also because they spend so much time underground. The US Geological Survey agrees: "Factors Affecting the Thermal Environment of Agassiz's Desert Tortoise (*Gopherus agassizii*) Cover Sites in the Central Mojave Desert during Periods of Temperature Extremes," by Jeremy S. Mack et al., *Journal of Herpetology* 49, no. 3 (September 2015), pp. 405–14.

101 The carapace of the desert tortoise: According to the Oneida Language and Cultural Centre, "The turtle's back is a significant symbol used in Iroquoian media. It represents the creation of Turtle Island, also known as the continent of North America, or turtle's back, or more accurately the 'Earth Grasper,' from our Creation Story." The Akta Lakota Museum and Cultural Center highlights the "13 Lakota Months" and notes that "the *keya* (turtle) has 13 large scales on its back, and 28 small scales around the shell. Because of these and other natural occurrences the *keya* became an important symbol." Evan Pritchard, founder of the Center for Algonquin Culture, notes in his book *Henry Hudson and the Algonquins of New York* (Tulsa, OK: Council Oak Books, 2009) that "in order to warn [Algonquin] people of a certain moment far into the future at which time they would have to make decisions that might affect the future of the planet, the [Algonquin] prophets provided a calendar of sorts. There was already a cycle of the day and the positions of the sun and moon; already a cycle of the month, which went from new moon to new moon; and there was a solar 'year' and a lunar 'year' marked out on the backs of 'moon turtles.'"

105 Ken Nagy, a biology professor emeritus: An engaging mix of science nerd and rugged Mojave Desert eccentric, Nagy personified a "type" I came across while reporting. But he's also unique, not to mention lucky. A veteran, Nagy enlisted in the navy in 1962: "We were just off the coast of Vietnam, our destroyer division doing plane guard detail behind an aircraft carrier—that's where you pick up the pilots that didn't hit the deck right, if they were still alive which they usually weren't. And all of a sudden we hear over the radio that part of our destroyer division is involved in something that got named the Gulf of Tonkin incident later on, which started the Vietnam War." An executive officer, who knew Nagy was slated to soon get off the ship and go back to college, made sure he got off when the ship docked in Japan to fully arm for battle.

105 Females usually dig a hole: In an update on the science since the initial juvenile desert tortoise releases, there has been a big problem with coyotes eating the 4.5-inch newly released young-sters, according to Nagy. The size was chosen to keep them safe from ravens. Coyotes go after tortoises of any size, but particularly juveniles—a danger that's been exacerbated by a boom in the coyote population and a drought that's made food supplies more scarce.

106 Nagy continues to be a serious scientist but with a morbid sense of humor: The "walking ravioli" quip pays tribute to Nagy's friend and fellow scientist David Morafka, who coined the term. Morafka was among the first to observe and then sound the alarm about crashing desert tortoise populations in the 1980s. Morafka initiated the first desert tortoise head-starting program, at Fort Irwin, and invited Nagy to join him. In honor of Morafka, who died in 2004 at the age of fifty-seven of pancreatic cancer, the Desert Tortoise Council offers the annual $2,000 David J. Morafka Award to help support research on and conservation of *Gopherus agassizii*. In the last few years of his life, Morafka focused on the effects of military maneuvers on lizard populations at Fort Irwin, as well as the biology of neonate desert tortoises.

107 Lydia Millet, a novelist and conservationist: It was with great emotion that I listened to Millet read "Good Grief: Style and Story in the Age of Extinction" at the public launch for UCLA's Laboratory for Environmental Narrative Strategies. The text is available in the online publication *LENS Magazine*: https://lensmagazine.org/good-grief-9087176b4a90. Millet's work also includes the exquisite and sometimes very funny trilogy on themes of death, loss, and blipping out for all eternity. The trilogy passes through *How the Dead Dream*, *Ghost Lights*, and *Magnificence*, but she had me at Andrew Jackson in those first pages of *How the Dead Dream*.

110 It's estimated that there are eighty-five thousand Mojave Desert tortoises remaining in the wild: In 2014, the US Fish and Wildlife Service estimated that there were eighty-five thousand range-wide in the desert tortoise conservation areas, a decline of 32 percent over a ten-year period. In "Desert Tortoises Gone Captive," *Sierra* (July 10, 2017), Daniel Rothberg quotes Kobbe Shaw, director of Tortoise Group, a tortoise-adoption organization in Nevada, estimating that "there could be as many as 200,000 captive desert tortoises roaming backyards in Las Vegas alone." https://www.sierraclub.org/sierra/desert-tortoises-gone-captive.

110 The jury is still out: Although still poorly understood, the preponderance of research on the homing and movement behaviors of Mojave Desert tortoises suggests that translocated animals move more overall than control groups. See "The Effects of Homing and Movement Behaviors on Translocation: Desert Tortoises in the Western Mojave Desert," by Danna Hinderle, Rebecca L. Lewison, Andrew D. Walde, et al., *Journal of Wildlife Management* 79, no. 1 (January 2015), pp. 137–47. Further, translocated desert tortoises in one study tended to "move greater distances in the first year after translocation than did residents, but their movement in the second or third year after translocation were indistinguishable from those of resident tortoises." "Translocation as a Conservation Tool for Agassiz's Desert Tortoises: Survivorship, Reproduction, and Movements," by Kenneth E. Nussear, Richard Tracy, Ronald W. Marlow, et al., *Journal of Wildlife Management* 76, no. 7 (September 2012), pp. 1341–53.

CHAPTER 6

120 The ecological interconnectedness of the region is best exemplified by the Santa Margarita River: *The Santa Margarita River: Cultural and Natural Resource Value* by Katharine Shapiro (Fallbrook, CA: Santa Margarita River Foundation, 1997) is a nice primer.

122 The Infantry Immersion Trainer: In a prepared statement for the hearing "Security Developments in the Areas of Responsibility of the US Southern Command, Northern Command, Africa Command, and Joint Forces Command," submitted to the US Senate Committee on Armed Services on March 18, 2009, General Mattis described the importance of immersion trainers: "The US Joint Forces Command is developing the Future Immersive Training Environment (FITE) to provide ground units from all services the same level of realistic training we provide in our aviation and maritime simulators in those domains. Today, our ground combat forces suffer more than 80 percent of our casualties and we can provide them with high-quality live, virtual, and constructive simulation capabilities to reduce this risk. Mixing brick and mortar surroundings with live actors and interactive virtual tools will provide unprecedented realism for our ground troops and better replicate the chaos of the 'first fights' so our youngest warriors are prepared for the tactical and ethical demands of combat among non-combatants."

128 The rules of their engagement originate: The beach and the nearby estuary had been heavily impacted prior to the biological opinion. Secondarily treated sewage effluent was released into the estuary from the 1940s through the early 1970s and, until 1970, the salt flats were used for tank training exercises.

134 "That's arundo. It's basically a habitat destroyer": *Arundo donax*, commonly known as giant reed, is currently considered to be one of the worst invasive species globally according to the article "Origin of the Invasive *Arundo donax* (Poaceae): A Trans-Asian Expedition in Herbaria" by Laurent Hardion, Régine Verlaque, Kristin Saltonstall, et al., *Annals of Botany* 114, no. 3 (September 2014) pp. 455–62. Where it constitutes native vegetation, the giant reed and the common reed, *Phragmites communis*, have been widely and productively utilized for thousands of years. I came across a wonderful description by Wilfred Thesiger in *The Last Nomad: One Man's Forty Year Adventure in the World's Most Remote Deserts, Mountains and Marshes* (New York: E.P. Dutton, 1979), p. 165: "The giant grass, which looked like a bamboo, grew densely....We passed villagers cutting young reeds as fodder for their buffaloes. In the bow of a canoe stood a naked boy, cutting the green shoots with a saw-edged sickle, then piling them dripping wet behind him. Beyond the curtain of the reeds I could hear talk and laughter." He refers to *Phragmites communis*, but several comprehensive studies also list *Arundo donax* as a species in the marshlands of Iraq during Thesiger's travels, around 1951. (In the 1980s, the marshlands were nearly obliterated by Saddam Hussein.)

139   Glyphosate-based herbicides have been used since the 1970s: Although California listed glyphosate as a chemical known to cause cancer in 2017 and the World Health Organization's International Agency for Research on Cancer announced in 2015 that the glyphosate was "probably carcinogenic," the US Environmental Protection Agency released a draft risk assessment report in December 2017 saying the agency found "no other meaningful risks to human health" when used according to label instructions.

140   "Any land manager will tell you": The first congressional oversight hearing on *Invasive Species Management on Federal Lands* was held on May 16, 2013, before the US House of Representatives Subcommittee on Public Lands and Environmental Regulation, Committee on Natural Resources. In his testimony, Paul Ries, associate deputy chief of State and Private Forestry for the US Forest Service, said: "Invasive species are among the most significant environmental and economic threats facing our nation." https://naturalresources.house.gov/calendar/eventsingle.aspx?EventID=333074.

145   Maintaining a "healthy tension": The phrase was used by Jeff Paull. Referring to the concept, he also noted that, "We make it sound like it's easy. It's not. There are months of tension between individual staff sections, larger mission objectives—all these issues....But when people commit their mind to it and commit to finding a real solution you end up with wonderful case studies.... There's a commitment all the way to the top for integration of mission requirements and stewardship requirements....From the top down it's, 'We are going to do both.'...With all of the major programs [at Pendleton], including services for training, facilities, logistics, security, there's a commitment that if we're going to do it we're going to do it right. We're going to do it the best. We're going to have showcase programs."

150   Many consider this a loophole in Section 7 of the Endangered Species Act: On the other side of the debate, many argue that Section 7 inhibits land use and economic development. Regarding the latter, research published in the peer-reviewed *Proceedings of* the *National Academy of Sciences of the United States of America* found that, in the previous seven years, and on over eighty-eight thousand US Fish and Wildlife Service consultations, no project had been stopped or even extensively altered as a result of Section 7. "Data Contradict Common Perceptions about a Controversial Provision of the US Endangered Species Act," by Jacob W. Malcolm and Ya-Wei Li, *Proceedings of the National Academy of Sciences of the United States of America*, 112, no. 52 (December 29, 2015), pp. 15844–49.

153 **"During my tours of duty"**: Thielen's courage in discussing his emotional trauma was astounding and gut-wrenching. As he related one experience: "You hear about people that had experiences and their brain just blocks it out. I actually had something like that happen to me when I was a sergeant. There was a helo [helicopter] crash in Korea and we lost twenty-seven people, and most of them were my peers and friends, a couple of guys that I worked with as a platoon sergeant. And I [long pause] kind of felt, I guess afterwards I would describe it as kind of I worked in shock; we were picking up the bodies and all this stuff off the hill. And then years later the movie *We Were Soldiers* came out, and they had that burn scene where they dropped the napalm—that triggered the burn scenes of those people that I was picking up from the helo, and it had just been repressed for years, like twenty-seven years."

ACKNOWLEDGMENTS

Many very busy military men and women, as well as their civilian colleagues, gave generously of their time and expertise in order to make this book possible. They helped me understand not only the science and technology related to their energy initiatives and their natural and cultural resources efforts but also the workings of the military world itself. I'd especially like to thank Jeff Paull, Camp Pendleton's deputy regional director for the Environmental Office. He was the first person I met on the first military installation I visited for this book, and he set a very high bar for all who came after. The Marine Corps' Tony Jackson also went above and beyond to help me up the learning curve, as did Ned McKinley, the California state director of the US Marine Corps West's Office of Government and External Affairs, and Rito Guerra, policy advisor for the Governor's Military Council. Rex Runyon at the Marine Corps Installations Command headquarters at the Pentagon smoothed the way for me with installation gatekeepers, none of whom would likely have been so welcoming had they just Googled my name. It was not always easy to jump through the public affairs hoops to get access to specific installations, but all those with whom I dealt got me what I needed. Ken Drylie at the army's Fort Irwin and Abigail Dredge at Camp Pendleton were especially helpful.

Thanks go as well to those in or associated with the conservation world who helped bring perspective and a reality check (organization names used for identification purposes only): Dan Silver at the Endangered Habitats League; Ileene Anderson at the Center for Biological Diversity; Zak Smith at Natural Resources Defense Council; Jenny Coyle and Curtis Seymour at the Energy Foundation; Carl Pope, author, with Michael Bloomberg, of *Climate of Hope: How Cities, Businesses, and Citizens Can Save the Planet*; Wade Crowfoot at the Water Foundation; and Bruce Hamilton and Kathryn Phillips at the Sierra Club. Others who helped sort out complicated issues related to the military, or simply inspire, include Major General Michael Lehnert and Jason Keyes. Stephanie Peek, also a great inspiration, tutored me on the visual art and history of camouflage.

This book would not have happened if not for Joan Hamilton, editor in chief at *Sierra* when I worked there. She trusted my judgment of people to profile for the magazine—people like Michael Lehnert—and wholly supported the push to highlight those not usually associated with the environmental movement but who are making important contributions. Her mentorship, encouragement, and constructive criticism were vital while at *Sierra*, and I'm additionally grateful that she did the same for me again when she read an early draft of this book. Thanks as well to Kerry Tremain for an early read. As for the finished product, although any errors are my responsibility alone, many thanks are due my diligent fact checker Sami Mericle.

Malcolm Margolin was vital to making this book a reality. His curious mind and hunger to avoid the ruts of conventional thinking and alliances animated the project from the start. I am grateful as well for the shaping guidance of Heyday's Gayle Wattawa and my wonderful editor Lindsie Bear. Two early chapter drafts I gave Lindsie were not good, but she told me so in such a way as to inspire the follow-up effort. What's more, she and I got this book done in a semi-timely fashion even though I got married and she had a baby in the midst of it. Welcome to the world, Maya.

I'm fortunate to have a family that indulges my passions. My parents read numerous chapter drafts and my father, a former utility company executive, helped with the complex issue of energy generation, distribution, and financing. My best and most put-upon reader has been my husband, Gregory Williams, who read some chapters so many times he could probably recite them in his sleep. Thank you for your love and support, and for your patience when the demands of this project were either keeping me on the road and away from home or making me crazy.

Finally, I'd like to give thanks to the barn owl and the blue jay that visited me, one toward the beginning and one at the end of this writing effort. In a dream I had shortly after teaming up with Heyday I was told by a barn owl that "the animals are watching." I was looking in the mirror but couldn't see myself; there was just a fluffy mass. The dream was so vivid that as I walked closer to the mirror I began to see in minute detail a bird's feathers, and just as I realized what that mass was the owl's head turned 180 degrees so I could see its piercing eyes; its words came low but very clear and precise. I don't usually even remember my dreams. And I've never before had an animal encounter, but a few months later—after a grueling day reporting at Twentynine Palms—I lay in a lawn chair looking up at the starry night sky when suddenly I heard the muffled *thwap* of a large bird landing on the fence post about three feet from my head. I moved only my eyes and there it was: the barn owl from my dream but in real life. We stared at each other for a long time, just as we did in the dream, until I had to blink. When my eyes opened it was gone. The blue jay visited the day I finished reporting. I was standing on my deck in San Francisco, exhausted and exhilarated, when the jay lighted on the wooden railing in front of me. I put out my hand; it hopped in place once or twice and then flew onto my fingers and stayed a few beats looking up at me before it took off into the dusk. All who know this story told me to keep it to myself. It's the perfect way to destroy what credibility I may have earned in these pages. But I'm also aware how entwined are the fates of humans and creatures, how intricate is the matrix that connects living things, and how little we truly understand any of it. So to hell with it. The birds get a shout-out.

ABOUT THE AUTHOR

Marilyn Berlin Snell is an independent journalist whose work focuses on the environment and politics. She was staff writer for *Sierra*, the magazine of the Sierra Club, from 2000 to 2008 and a founding director of the magazine's Investigative Journalism Project. Her freelance work has appeared in publications including the *New York Times, Mother Jones, The Nation*, and *Discover*. She conducted one of the last interviews with Nobel climate scientist Stephen Schneider for the *New Republic* before his untimely death.

green press

INITIATIVE

Heyday is committed to preserving ancient forests and natural resources. We elected to print this title on 30% post consumer recycled paper, processed chlorine free. As a result, for this printing, we have saved:

10 Trees (40' tall and 6-8" diameter)
4 Million BTUs of Total Energy
846 Pounds of Greenhouse Gases
4,590 Gallons of Wastewater
308 Pounds of Solid Waste

Heyday made this paper choice because our printer, Thomson-Shore, Inc., is a member of Green Press Initiative, a nonprofit program dedicated to supporting authors, publishers, and suppliers in their efforts to reduce their use of fiber obtained from endangered forests.

For more information, visit www.greenpressinitiative.org

Environmental impact estimates were made using the Environmental Defense Paper Calculator. For more information visit: www.papercalculator.org.